Mental Toughness for Young Athletes

Volume 2 "Grit: The Secret Mindset Hack"

Moses and Troy Horne

Want to go to the next level?
Visit mentaltoughnesspdf.com **to learn more!**

CONTENTS

You The Superhero

You are the hero! You! Not that girl over there or that guy over there. **YOU** are the hero of this story called your youth sports life. Everything that you have been looking for outside of yourself is hiding there inside you. The grit that you are looking for to take your in-game performance to the next level is there inside of you. The mental toughness that you are looking for to dominate in that same game is there inside you. The confidence, the strength, the ability to win is all right there inside of you. You just need a little help to pull it out of you. That's why you are here. Something inside of you said that you had enough of not making it happen.

Something inside of you said that it's time to be more. That is why this book spoke to you. This book is your lost scrolls, it's your hidden message buried inside the secret lair. This book is your hero's guide to your greater self, and I am super excited that you picked it up. Let's get you going on your journey to your greater self. Clearly, it's time and you are ready for the change.

Every hero has a set of villains that they have to defeat. In this book we are going to give you the tools that you need to defeat your evil villains. For the sake of this book, I am going to name them all Villain #1. Why? Because we seem to assign importance or less importance to things when they are labeled one, two, three, four and so on. I don't want you to do that. I don't want you to think that one villain is less important than the other. I don't want you to think "Well, I got villain number one, two and three under control. I don't need to worry about four or five." Nope. They will all need to be defeated in order for you to win. Every single one.

I'm talking about Villain #1 Time Management and Training, Villain #1 Understanding The Journey, Villain #1 The Sacrifice Winning Requires, Villain #1 The Absence of History, Villain #1 The Power Of The Spoken Word and Villain #1 The Mentor-less Quest. Speaking of mentors, every hero has a bunch of guides along their path. Each guide helps them pull out the hero inside of them that is destined to save the world. Luke Skywalker had his Uncle Owen and his Aunt Beru, then he had Yoda, Obi-Wan, Han Solo, Princess Leia, and even Darth Vader as guides along his path. Yes, even the bad guys can be guides along your path.

Prince T'Challa of the Black Panther had his mother and father King T'Chaka and Queen Ramonda, his sister princess Shuri, his uncle Prince Zuri, his friend Nakia, tribe leader M'Baku, the villain The Klaw, and even his cousin Erik Kilmonger. Every hero has many guides that teach them along the way. My hope is that you will allow us to be a couple of those guides for you on this part of your journey. We've been where you are, and we want to help you get to where you want to go. As you go through the pages of this book think of this as your step-by-step guide to your next level of mental toughness. Think of us as your Yoda and Obi-Wan preparing you for your next big battle. Read every page and mark every lesson that sticks out to you. They stick out to you for a reason.

Be aware that at different times in your journey, different parts of this book will call out to you. That is why it is important that you read every page. It is a living and breathing document for the living and breathing sports journey that you are taking. Keep these lessons close to your mind and revisit them whenever you have a temporary struggle along the way. Remember you are going to have to defeat all of your Villain #1s when they show up. Your journey will require that you have grit. Your journey will require that the grit that you have be used in moments of fear and doubt. We know because that is what the journey has taught us. Lucky for you, you have something that we wish that we would have had. You have this book. It's here for you. No hero wins alone. No hero succeeds without a guide and no hero avoids the struggles that come with being a hero. You can do this. We see the hero inside of you and apparently that hero is ready to come out. Nothing happens by accident.

Welcome to your journey to your mental toughness self part two. As the hero of your story know that mastery will come just in time for life to throw you another curveball. The difference between now and the past is that you will be ready for the change up when it happens. So buckle up. We look forward to helping you win. Thank you for allowing us to be a small part of your journey. Let's get started hero. Your journey, your team and your destiny is waiting for you.

Introduction

"There are levels, kid."

L et me tell you a story about a high school basketball player and his dad. They are probably a lot like you and your family. They went to the gym a lot, practiced a lot, did a lot of drills and all of that stuff. They were doing everything they could to be the best that they could. They even had a podcast back in the day where they interviewed Hall of Famers to ask them questions about sports and mental toughness. They interviewed, Chauncey Billups, Earl Boykins and even KOBE FREAKIN' BRYANT. You can hear it for yourself on iTunes or Stitcher; just type "Hoopchalk Basketball Podcast" into Google, and the Google bot will do the rest. YA WELCOME!

Well, as the story goes, it was your typical day in your typical high school basketball gym in anywhere in the world basketball land. I (the dad in this story) was in the gym with

Moses (the young athlete in this story). We were checking out his future high school basketball team. They were working out in the gym and we were there so that he could see what practice was going to be like at the next level. Even in that moment we were getting his mind prepared for the future. We were doing the old "sit on the extremely uncomfortable bleachers and watch a team practice" thing. When "it" happened!

What I'm about to share with you happened so quietly that it could have easily been missed if I wasn't paying attention. So pay attention, because this story is gold! It was so profound that it has stuck with me ever since. I mean, I remembered it for this book, so there's that. Here's how it all went down. You're gonna love this!

That day in the gym there was a pretty good high school basketball player playing King of the Court with his teammates. This kid was running through his teammates one after another. He had just won back to back games of King of the Court. Needless to say, he was "smelling himself a little bit", as my dad used to say, and rightly so. I mean after all, he was beating everyone.

Now, for those of you who don't know. King of the Court is a series of one-on-one basketball games where the player who scores or the player who stops her or him from scoring gets to stay on the court. Basically, you keep playing until you go through the entire line of players. The only way to become the new king/queen of the court is to stop the person with the ball (or current king/queen) from scoring, or you can score on the defender in front of you. Score on everyone in line without losing once and you win the game, becoming the new queen/king of the court. In the series of one-on-one games, the loser goes to the back of the line to wait for their turn to try to stop the kid on the court from scoring. Hope I didn't over explain that even though I probably did.

Well, after this certain player's third or fourth round of going through all of the players, he decided to challenge the high school basketball team's assistant coach who was in the gym at the time. At first, the coach shrugged it off and kept cleaning the gym. "You know you can't guard me, Coach," called out the young high school athlete. It was after practice, so everyone was basically just puttering around. Some of the kids were putting on their slides, and some of the kids were just scrolling on their phones as they waited for a text from their ride home. You know, doing kid stuff. Everyone was in relax mode, but this kid wouldn't stop calling out the coach. "He doesn't want to play me because he's scared," the young athlete continued.

Now, there is only so much of this that any person can take, and as a parent sitting in the gym, I knew this young athlete calling out a grown man would only last so long without a response. I was correct. The kid kept going at the coach. He was pretty persistent; I'll give him that. After what seemed like a fifteen-minute onslaught, the coach said, "All right, bet. Check up."

I knew the kid was in for a beat down!

The other kids clapped them up and the coach put down the dust mop. He was definitely preparing for the lesson he was about to teach. Cheers of "YEEAHHH!" rang throughout the gym. The other kids in the gym thought they were about to see a good match. However, I knew they were about to see the dismantling of youth confidence.

You see, in the coach's voice was the sound of someone who already knew what the outcome was going to be. It was the sound of Michael Phelps staring at Chad Le Clos after Chad started shadow boxing in front of him before their 200-meter semifinals race in 2016. Yes, a stare can have a sound. Take a look at the picture of it on the free download that comes with this book. In the coach's voice was the sound of Bradley Beale telling his AAU team that none of them could guard him and that none of them were going to take his job. Video is also over on the free download I made for you.

Yeah, by the way, this book comes with a free download. It cost me a bit of time and money to make, have designed and stuff, but it's free for you. There is a lot of stuff in there that you are going to want to see and hear. I'm talking about videos and audios and more good stuff that will help you along your journey. It's really going to help you apply all of the information you are about to learn… and did I mention that it's free? There's a lot here in this book. The free download makes it easier to digest. Go and get it at mentaltoughnesspdf.com. Go do it now while you're thinking about it.

All right, back to the story…

There was a lot in those few words that the coach said to the high school athlete. In the coach's voice was the sound of someone who had been tested, failed a lot in the past but kept trying. His voice was filled with the calm, confident energy of someone who had learned how to come out on top against difficult odds. His voice had the sound of someone who had learned how to win as a result of losing. It was the sound of someone who had grit.

Now, don't get me wrong, the high school player was definitely a good player, but he was missing that one ingredient that makes good players great players. He was missing the determination that comes with having had to struggle. He was missing the confidence that comes with having been tested and failed over and over again! He was missing the calmness that comes from having tasted defeat over and over again. He was missing the confidence that comes with the decision to keep going until you win. He was missing the strength that comes from having gone through the fire. Like I said before, he was missing the thing that you bought this book for: He was missing grit!

The assistant coach stepped up to the top of the key, passed the ball to the young high school player, and said, "You can have the ball first." The high school basketball player, let's call him Matt, grinned and went into his triple threat stance. He jabbed left, then jabbed right. Then he drove past the assistant coach and on to the basket. The coach sat back and let Matt blow by him. Matt made his way to the basket for what he probably thought was about to be an easy layup. However, to his surprise, he was met with the sound of having his shot blocked off of the backboard. SMACK! The sound of the ball bouncing off of the backboard rang throughout the gym like a bell as it flew back onto the court. "Zero, zero," the coach said as he walked back to the top of the key. One of the other players in the gym got the ball from mid court and passed it back to the coach. "Check up," the coach said as he passed the ball back to Matt.

After that, you can imagine how it went. The basketball coach beat Matt pretty easily, scoring basket after basket with ease. It was almost like Matt wasn't even there. Just like I had predicted, the coach beat Matt soundly, and he did it without having to say a word. Now, don't get me wrong, a lot of players with grit talk trash, and we'll get to that in a minute, but they usually only do it with people they perceive as real competition. There are a lot of things that go with trash talking and I can guarantee that you probably don't know them. Don't worry, you will after you finish this book.

The coach in this story knew that Matt wasn't real competition, so he just beat him. The other players on the sidelines did all the trash-talking for him. Most of the time, players with grit won't talk trash to people they don't see as serious competition. That is, unless it's Kobe. Kobe talked trash to everyone. HA! He was a special kind of player. He was different!

Pro Tip #1: (Outside of Kobe) If a player with grit is ever talking trash to you, it's because he or she sees you as a formidable competitor. Take it as a compliment and bark back!

Pro Tip #2: Players with grit usually won't talk trash first. Players with grit will usually go quiet first, like the lion stalking their prey. During that time, they are sizing you up for the kill. They are studying your tendencies. They are finding your weaknesses. They are preparing to pounce on your neck. You know the part in the hero movie just before the good guy is about to fight the bad guy? What are they doing? They are usually sitting there quietly assessing the situation. I put a video example of it on the download for you so that you can see what I am talking about. On the flip side, players **WITHOUT** grit usually talk first. Kind of like the bad guy in the film who has the upper hand for a moment, but then talks too long and ends up getting his butt kicked. That used to always drive me crazy in the movies. The bad guy always talked just before the big fight. You'd they would learn. I was always like, "Stop talking bro! Just beat the hero now while he's down." But they never do. Don't be the bad guy in your film. Less talking, more assessing the situation.

Part one of assessing your opponent is recognizing if they are talking or not talking. Talking first means they are worried, concerned or overly-confident. That means, for the first round at least, they are going to be apprehensive and a little slower than usual. Talking opponents are usually careless because they are worried about getting beat. Kobe even went silent before playing Lil' Bow Wow. LiL' BOW WOW GUYS!

He went Mamba gritty with a 5-foot rapper named Lil' Bow Wow who didn't even play pro basketball. That's CRAZY! It's also in a video on the download. At the 22-second mark, Bow Wow is doing the bad guy talking thing. Kobe sees this happening and then proceeds to respond knowing that the dismantling is about to happen. Notice that he doesn't talk until **AFTER** he recognizes that Bow Wow has started talking. In that moment, the Mamba realizes Bow Wow is not the gritty one in this situation. Man, that guy was a master at this gritty mental toughness stuff. Keep an eye out. It's a subtle difference, but it makes all the difference. (By the way, I know that movies are all written for the bad guy to lose. I just think this is a moment where life imitates art.) Now let's get back to our story...

The coach didn't talk trash to Matt because he didn't think of him as competition. To be honest, he had probably already sized him up when Matt was playing King of the Court with the other players. That's what gritty players do. Like I said, the journey never ends. Once a mamba, always a mamba. For gritty athletes, EVERY moment is a moment to evaluate any and all possible threats in the room, on the field or on the court. Gritty players stay in grit mode. They are always assessing their surroundings and their competition. The coach was probably thinking things like this as Matt was winning against the younger players.

- *He likes to go left.*

- *He finishes low off the glass.*

- *He doesn't like to shoot the ball.*

- *When he shoots the ball, he does this move or that move first.*

You get the idea. All this was happening while he was cleaning up the gym, putting the basketballs away and sweeping the floor. Gritty athletes are always evaluating the situation. Like Denzel in the clip over on the download. Always! Matt talked a lot, and he talked first because he was going off of current success; he clearly had not been tested. He had not experienced loss on a large scale. He had not been challenged. The coach easily beat him, and when they were done, he simply turned to Matt and said, "There are levels, kid."

If you are reading this book, hopefully you have already read the first book *Mental Toughness for Young Athletes*. If not, uh... you need to go and get that book. It is the foundation for everything you are going to learn in this book. Go to https://amzn.to/3aPpknZ to get your copy if you are reading the ebook, or just go to Amazon and search "Mental Toughness for Young Athletes." We're probably still number one.

If you are confused as to which one is ours, just look for the one that looks a lot like the cover of this book. If you don't have it, go get it right now. It is super important! You are going to want to have that book and its information as a part of your tool kit. It's your black belt certification for all of this mental toughness stuff. This is your second-degree black belt certification. Don't go forward with your second-degree black belt if you don't have your blackbelt. Cool? Cool.

Now, for those of you who have the first book and have already read it, you will have a really great understanding of the building blocks of this thing called "mental toughness." You already have the eight exercises that help you strengthen your mental toughness mindset muscles, so you are well on your way! Now it's time to become elite in all this mental toughness stuff. Now is the time for you to become **#different**. In the next few pages, you are going to move from your black belt in mental toughness to your second-degree black belt. As the coach said to the defeated high school athlete after handing him that "L" in the gym that day, "There are levels, kid." It's time for you to level up.

In this book, there will be sections written by me, and there will be sections co-written and read by Moses over on the audiobook version. We did this so you can get the athlete's perspective and the parent's/coach's perspective in the same book. We noticed that you all liked when we did that in the last book, so we did it again. No matter who you are—parent, coach, or athlete—you should be aware of both perspectives. Don't skip! Read it all. You want both! Now that we've got that out of the way, let's get started on your second degree blackbelt in mental toughness. I'm excited for you! Let's GO!

CHAPTER 1

Let's Grit It Started

Bruce Lee Mentals
(Player Perspective)

Welcome to Chapter 1. This is your step one guide to the confidence that comes from earning your grit stripes. As my dad says to me whenever we are joking around about how to do something, "Are you going to talk about it or be about it?" That basically means, show me instead of telling me. Be about it. Show, don't tell. That's what grit makes you do.

Grit is that relaxed but focused Kobe Bryant stare that sends opponents running the other way. Grit is the look on the face of a focused lion or tiger when hunting prey they know they are going to catch. It looks like Denzel Washington in the fight scene over on the free download. If you ever watch a film of a born predator hunting its prey, you will notice that its face relaxes, its body prepares, and its voice gets quiet. Lions don't roar when they hunt. They quietly stalk. They roar (or talk lion trash) when they want other lions to know they run this part of the grasslands. Learn what they already learned from some of those hard life lion lessons.

A young lion learns grit after a couple nights without food. For some of them, it might have even meant starving to death. Did you know that lions only eat every three to four days? Imagine a young lion out on the grassy plains of Africa. He just left the pride (or was kicked out because he was too old), and now he has to fend for himself. He doesn't have the pride to help him hunt for food. He has to get it all on his own. The young lion spots a gazelle on the horizon. He starts dreaming of not being hungry and aggressively starts to run towards his possible future meal.

Keep in mind, he probably hasn't eaten in three to four days, so there's that. He's pretty hungry. What happens next is going to change his life one way or another. Either he's going to eat or he's going to have a long night with an empty stomach... again!

This lion is new to hunting, so he just runs towards the gazelles hoping to catch one of them. Any one of them will do. He's literally starving to death and is probably feeling pretty weak. He is using all the energy he's got to get some dinner. The gazelles, who are always on high alert because they are gazelles, hear him coming and run off. Why? Because gazelles are always looking around for any oncoming threat. If they don't, they could die. Once they see the young lion running towards them, they are out of there. The reward for **NOT** being stealthy is another night of hunger for our young lion friend and another day of being hangry.

His growling stomach that night, and possibly the next couple of nights, would be his first taste of what it's like not to lead with the quiet observation that grit requires. Either way, the lion must quickly learn to adapt or he could die of hunger. The lion gets smarter and grittier because of his losses, not because of his wins. A couple of nights without dinner has a way of making you figure it out. That's for sure. I had a couple of lion grit moments.

When I first arrived at Oak Hill, I played a couple of the ranked guys that were there. When I first got there I could barely move on the court without having the ball stolen. There I was, one of the top basketball players in my home state of Colorado, and I couldn't even dribble the ball against some of the guys. I had a choice to make. I could quit and not get better or I could do what Kobe did and get to work. I decided to get to work.

The choice wasn't hard. It was either keep playing, develop grit and learn to win because you aren't afraid to lose, or go home and stay average. They definitely weren't going to let me win. I was going to have to earn it. Long story short, I left there the third leading scorer on my team for the season. That's what grit will do for you. When you are put in situations where you can possibly fail, grit will show you who you really are. It will bring out the champion that lies within you, or it will bring out the other person. Either way, you get to learn from your experiences. If you get nothing else from this book, get this: You only fail when you stop trying. You only lose when you don't get back up and go for it again.

Life is a series of opportunities. Gritty people take advantage of the opportunities despite the possibility of failure. Gritty people are familiar with failure. They actually seek it out. Gritty people will play the game not worried about failing because they will keep playing the game until they win. Gritty people understand that failure is just a learning opportunity. Failing is your chance to learn what not to do. You know what Thomas Edison said when he was struggling to make the light bulb work. He said, *"I have not failed. I've just found 10,000 ways that won't work"*.

Have you tried and failed at anything ten thousand times? I'm pretty sure that the answer is no. Well, that is what it takes obviously. It's time to be so committed to your goal that you are willing to fail ten thousand times to get it right. Learn from any and all of your failures, get back up and try again, rinse and repeat until you win. It's really that easy.

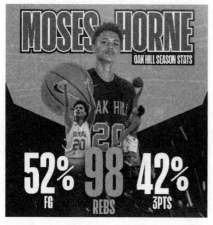

Because of that kind of commitment, I went on to become a team captain as a sophomore. I had a 26-point game on 69% shooting against a college basketball team, and I was only fifteen at the time. Some of those guys had beards. Some of them were as much as seven years older than I was. All of this happened with a 15-year-old, now 16-year-old kid, and all of this because of second-degree-blackbelt-level grit.

Now, like anything that you set out to do, there are going to be problems and roadblocks. Before you get all excited about the process and about how you are going to rock this next level of mental toughness, let's go over those roadblocks that are waiting for you on your journey. We need to do this before you get going so the roadblocks don't blindside you on your way towards your second-degree mental toughness blackbelt gritty self!

I Got 99 Problems...

Here are some of the problems you will face on your way to finding your new gritty self. You're gonna be surprised by the last one. Don't skip ahead to read the last one. Just read them in order. I know you thought about it.

Problem #1: I don't live in a place that has gritty people.

Benjamin Hardy writes in his book *Willpower Doesn't Work,* and classic motivational speaker Zig Ziglar says in almost all of his motivational lectures…

"You become part of what you are around."

The problem a lot of people have is believing they don't live in a place that makes gritty people. I know, because I was one of those people. A lot of young athletes feel like they are not in a community or a place that supports high-level competition. I totally get it! Unless you live in a highly competitive area. You feel like your city or state isn't one that makes a lot of pros or high level players. You feel like you don't have access to high levels of competition in your community. I get it. There is a way around that. We'll talk about that in a minute, but for now let's talk about what you can do right now today.

Most people don't have mentors or surroundings that create a gritty lifestyle. I mean, if you are reading this book, you probably aren't living in poverty like the poverty in São Paulo where Pelé grew up. You probably aren't kicking a sock filled with newspaper instead of a soccer ball when you play soccer with your friends like Pelé had to. That was Pelé's grit-making environment. Most of the greats that we know did the spartan thing at some point in their life. Having to figure a lot of hard things out at a young age makes you a little grittier than most.

You probably aren't playing tennis on the broken-down courts of Compton, California like Venus and Serena Williams were. By the way, did you know their dad Richard Williams moved them to Compton on purpose? He wanted them to have to deal with life in a gritty situation. That's next-level mental toughness coaching for sure. You probably aren't familiar with gang shootings, or gangs at all, like they were. You're probably not working on your gymnastics on old equipment in a dark and dusty gym in 1980s Russia like many of the Olympic gold medalists were during Russia's gymnastic dominance.

We know you guys, we talk to some of you via email and stuff if you are a part of our group. Basically, if you are reading this book, your life is probably not too challenging as far as all of that stuff goes. I mean, you might have a tough day here and there where you get unfollowed on social media, or you don't get as many points as you thought you should in a game, or something like that. Maybe you don't get as many likes on a post as you had hoped, but you're not wondering if what you're doing right now is going to cause you to miss your next meal. You're not worried that your walk home is going to put your life in danger. You're probably not dodging gangs as you walk down the street or anything like that. Your father isn't fighting gang members so they will leave you alone while you practice tennis.

Man, Richard Williams is a beast! He actually did that. He fought gang members who were bothering Serena and Venus while they practiced. He lost a lot of times, but his grit had them showing up the next day to practice again despite the gangs. Eventually the gang members saw that he wasn't going to stop helping his kids, and they left him alone. That's another story for another book, though. Let's get back to you.

Your "tough days" when you lose a follower or whatever, are probably not your normal everyday life, and even if it is, hopefully you can see that your life really ain't that bad. You are seeing that right? Ok. Good! Right now, you're probably thinking,

"Whelp, time to give this book away because my life isn't that bad or rough. I'm doomed. I will never be as gritty as those sports icons."

Well, hold on there Panickin Skywalker, no need to worry just yet. Grit is still right around the corner. You just have to know where to look. Here's how I know that becoming "grittier" is a possibility for you.

One of the grittiest people to ever play the game of basketball grew up middle-class and pretty sheltered. That was what he said to me in his own words. He wasn't worried about much. He grew up pretty privileged as growing up goes. I mean, his dad was a former NBA player and then went on to play pro in Italy. How do I know? Because I interviewed this person, and he told me this himself. Kobe Bean Bryant was a shy, middle-class kid who lacked a lot of confidence when he was first starting out. Those are his words, not mine. I put a link to the interview I did with him in the free download that comes with this book. Yup, there is still a free download with some support materials waiting for you over at mentaltoughnesspdf.com. Including my interview with Kobe. Go get it! Still free. All of this to say that you're in good company. The Mamba didn't grow up in a gritty environment. However, if you want your mamba card, you are going to need to do what he did to get what he got.

You know what other gritty icons grew up middle-class and even upper-middle-class? Do you know what gritty athletes missed growing up in a "tough" environment but found their way towards their iconic gritty selves? Wayne Gretzky, Chris Paul, Michael Phelps, Steph Curry, Diana Taurasi, Tom Brady, Missy Franklin, Barry Bonds, Michelle

Wie West, Mark McGwire, Michael Jordan, Sue Bird, Raven Saunders, Bubba Wallace and countless other athletes who are known for their grit. I am telling you this to show you that not growing up in a tough situation is not a problem anymore. Not being around what many would call your classic grit-creating people, places or experiences can be something that you can overcome. I'm gonna show you how in this book, but before we do all that, let's address two more problems that you will probably face along the way.

Problem #2: I don't have a grit coaching mentor.

The funny thing is that you probably do. The one thing all these gritty icons had in common was they all had a mentor who basically kicked their butt. They all had their Mr. Miyagi who would call them out on their shtuff and push them when they needed to be pushed. They all had their own no-nonsense Cus D'amato. They all had someone who brought the grit out of them. They at least watered the seed and helped it grow. You may be thinking, *I don't have anyone like that around me.* Let me explain something that you probably don't realize.

The Truth About Adult Mentors: Explained

Most trainers, mentors and coaches are great grit-creating people by nature. The issue is that they are withholding the grit part from your coaching or training. They aren't just doing it to you, they are doing it to pretty much every other young athlete. Why? Because most athletes can't handle the process that it takes to become gritty. Most athletes want you to give them what is called the "compliment sandwich," and that stuff doesn't make you gritty. The compliment sandwich goes something like this:

Coach: Hey, Marvin.

Marvin: Yup. (Note to self: True young athletes looking for grit say "Yes, sir/ma'am" or "Yes, Coach," not yup.)

Coach: You are doing really well with blah, blah, blah.

Marvin: Thanks, Coach.

Coach: You know, I've been thinking... You might want to take another look at your blah, blah, blah. You could really do that better if you focused on it. I think it could really help your game.

Marvin: No problem, Coach. I will look into it.

Coach: Cool. Yeah, like I said, you are really great at blah, blah, and I know if you get this right you will be even better all around.

Did you follow that? Basically, the compliment sandwich opens with a compliment, puts the criticism or direction in the middle, and then follows that up with another compliment. It feels good to the tender-hearted and puts a smile on their face. However, it ain't how you get better, and it definitely isn't how you become a mamba.

Gritty mentors don't have time for all that! To be honest, they aren't good at all this new, soft mentoring stuff. If you want grit to become a part of your life, you are going to need to put on your big girl and boy pants and understand that criticism and direction are not about how bad you are. Direct criticism is not an assault on your whole human existence. Direct, unsugar-coated direction is not meant to make you feel bad about yourself. Criticism and direction are there to show you where you are right now in a straightforward, no nonsense way so that you can fix it quickly and get on with getting better. As my dad says to me, "Don't be concerned when they are talking to you. They are telling you things because they believe in you and think that you can fix it and get better. Be concerned when they stop talking to you."

That being said, most trainers and coaches are more than capable of giving you the classic grit-creating training. However, they don't give you what you need to be gritty because most people can't handle it. As a matter of fact, I think it is safe to say that a majority of the population can't handle it. That's why you can probably count on one hand the great athletes in your sport who are considered gritty. The people who could help you achieve your goal of being "grittier" don't have time for all that indirect, compliment sandwich stuff. They need to give it to you straight or not at all. They aren't made to tell you what you want to hear so that you can feel happy about your achievements. They only do this non-gritty style of coaching now so they don't have to deal with the backlash of possibly losing your business.

Do they want to do this gritless type of coaching with you? No! However, they have learned to be less gritty when they coach. They have learned that most young athletes will leave or go to another trainer or program if they are hard on them. So, in order to have a successful business, they soften their training and give you the training without the bite. They give you the "feel good" training without the teeth, and yes, without the grit. By default, you usually end up feeling good but being average.

If you really want the real-deal-Holyfield training that not only makes you grittier but also makes you great, you are going to need to give them permission to give you that real-deal, old school, get your grit on training. It's on the secret hidden menu, kinda like the animal-style burger at In-N-Out. Ya welcome!

The real-deal, hardcore, grit-making training really is the good stuff and the only way to be next-level great. So, grow a thick skin, understand that they are directing and criticizing you because they believe in you. Then, get to work. Hey, if they tell you that you suck now, know that you won't always suck. Just keep working, eventually they will say "you're ok." That's grit coach code for I'm proud of you.

Keep in mind that along the way, you might have to remind them that you are okay with having them be direct with you. They've probably been burned a time or two by young athletes who said they wanted to have them be direct and authentic only to have the kid crumble under the pressure. Make sure that you keep your fluff radar up. If you start sensing that your new grit mentor is going soft on you, you might need to remind them that you want your training with a cup of grit (hold the sugar). The one thing you have to remember is that most trainers who work with you think you're pretty good at what you do. That's why they are working with you. Any criticism from a tough coach is given with the understanding that just because you suck now doesn't mean you are going to suck forever. Gritty people have what is called a "growth mindset". Time for you to get one if you don't have one already.

The Growth Mindset: Explained

"There's another mindset in which these traits are not simply a hand you're dealt and have to live with, always trying to convince yourself and others that you have a royal flush when you're secretly

worried it's a pair of tens. In this mindset, the hand you're dealt is just the starting point for development. This growth mindset is based on the belief that your basic qualities are things you can cultivate through your efforts."

—Carol Dweck, author of *Mindset*

Carol Dweck wrote this in her book *Mindset* about a mentality that she calls the growth mindset. Basically, she says that there are two types of mindsets in this world: a fixed mindset and a growth mindset. The fixed mindset says that you are born with all the tools you will ever have. The fixed mindset offers limited beliefs like, one must be born with 'it,' or that certain people just have talent because they were born with the right genes or in the right circumstances. The fixed mindset believes that you are what you are, and you can never change it. This is NOT the mindset of the greats we see in the Hall of Fame.

I have interviewed a lot of pros and a couple Hall of Famers, and some future Hall of Famers. All of them have said that the difference between them and everyone else was hard work. None of them said, "Well, I was just born with it." They all said that, in the beginning, they were not seen as great. In some cases, they say they weren't even seen as good. However, they kept working and growing. All of the people my dad and I interviewed had what Carol Dweck calls the growth mindset, all of them.

The growth mindset says that any skill can be learned or acquired. Countless icons in the past, present and future will tell you stories about how they were the worst player on the team at some point. They will all tell you about how they were overlooked and underestimated at some point. What did they do? They worked on whatever skill they were horrible at and made their weakness their strength. Want to be gritty? Have a growth mindset. Understand that any criticism is an observation of where you are now. It doesn't mean you are going to be there forever. Growth mindset is key! Get one NOW! Last but not least...

Problem #3: YOU!

Confidence in yourself is key, but confidence is not easy to come by in the beginning. The great thing about confidence is that it can be earned and learned. How do you learn confidence, you ask? You get to work doing the thing you are not confident doing. You do it so often. You do it as well as you can until you can't miss. Want to be a great three-point shooter? Shoot three-pointers until you can't miss. Want to be a great batter in baseball? Practice hitting until you can't miss. Want to be a great scorer in soccer? Shoot on goal until you can't miss. It's really that simple. As Kobe said in our interview, the more you do something, the more confident you become in your ability to do it. Want to be confident about something? Keep working on your weaknesses until you can do it in your sleep. Repetition breeds confidence, kind of like walking. Think about it this way:

When you were a baby, every step was a big deal to you. Every little shuffle forward was a big moment to you and your mom and dad, but after doing it every day, walking became super easy, and you became super confident. Now you get up and walk around without even thinking about it. Your mom or dad calls your name, and you just stand up and walk to the kitchen or down the stairs without giving it a second thought.

They don't celebrate you taking each step like they did when you were a one-year-old. You are an expert at walking now. You have done it so much that you don't think about it. Heck, nobody thinks about it. That is the power of repetition. Remind yourself of this fact whenever you start to feel a lack of confidence creeping in. If you are feeling a lack of confidence, then you haven't done whatever it is you are not confident about enough times. More reps necessary. Get to work!

Another **"YOU"** problem that many people have is their own self talk. We all say things to ourselves that we would never say to our worst enemy. Go over some of the things you have said to yourself about yourself in the last four hours. Now ask yourself if your friend would have said that to you, would you still be his or her friend? The answer is probably **NO**! In some cases, you might have even asked them to step outside to handle it. That being said, before you go any further, I want you to apologize to yourself. I know it sounds corny, but you gotta do it. Do it right now! Then, I want you to tell yourself how awesome you are. I'm being serious. I want you to start doing that every day! Yeah, every day!

Every day you need to tell yourself that you are absolutely amazing. I mean, every day you have probably told yourself that you were horrible in one way or another. So you gotta make up for all of your own negative programming. You don't have to say it out loud if you don't want to, but you do have to say it, AND you do have to say it every day. Look. You are your greatest problem when it comes to your success, and on the flip side, you are also your greatest solution. It has always been you, and it will always be you. Mastering you and your confidence is the real game here. As the African Proverb says...

"When there is no enemy within, the enemies outside cannot hurt you."

All you need to do to crush this last problem is start talking better to yourself about yourself. Keep saying what you want to happen and how you want things to be, and they will become your new reality. You've been talking crazy to yourself for years. Time to talk to yourself like you would your best friend. You are the only person who will always be with you. Always! Everywhere you go you will always be there with you! You deserve to be your best friend.

CHAPTER 2

It Was Scary in The Beginning

(Parent/Coach Perspective)

Everything is scary in the beginning. Like all human beings, we started off as frightened little babies. When we were little, we were afraid of the dark. We were afraid of loud noises. We were afraid of sudden movements. We were afraid of pretty much everything! As babies, we lived our lives like the gazelles on the plains of Africa from our earlier story. We were terrified and on high alert all the time. Then, life happens, and we become a little less scared of loud noises and things like that. As we get older, we realize that the lights being turned off will not hurt us. Believe it or not, even as a little baby, we were all developing our mental grit muscles.

As a young kid, there were a lot of things that helped me become more and more gritty. One of them was going off to college by myself and having to figure all that stuff out. After that, it was going to Los Angeles by myself to pursue my dream of becoming a professional musician. Driving into that city for the first time was pretty scary. Moving to Los Angeles at twenty years old with only $1,500 dollars to your name will wake you up pretty quick.

For many people, just getting older is a real grit-maker. At each stage in life, you reach a new point of understanding. In some way, shape or form, your back is up against the wall, and you have no choice but to go forward. Dwayne "The Rock" Johnson talks about this all the time when he talks about how he started his journey to superstardom. (Video of him talking about it on the free download.)

As the story goes, Dwayne was feeling on top of the world. Life was going great. He had a scholarship at The University of Miami playing football. Miami was winning national championship after national championship. They were kind of a big deal. Then it came time for him to graduate. People all around him were having success and getting drafted to the NFL. The Rock was thinking, *Man, I'm a bad mother…!* He was definitely in the right place at the right time and on the right team. It's kind of crazy because you can actually see a young Dwayne "The Rock" Johnson in ESPN's documentary *The U*! He was on a team with NFL Hall of Famers Warren Sapp and Ray Lewis. He was right there in the right gritty environment with the top-level guys, and football still didn't work out for him.

He tells a story about how Warren Sapp walked right up to him one day and said to him, "Yo, Dew, I'm going to take your spot." The Rock then turned to him and said, "You're not taking my spot." And then Warren Sapp proceeded to take his spot. Warren Sapp, a kid who had grown up in a gritty situation, had things The Rock didn't have yet. He had that voice of the coach from the earlier story. He had the determination that came from having his back against the wall. He had grit. Dwayne didn't have that level of grit or resolve yet, at least not on the level that he needed it at that point in his life.

The season ended, and Dwayne didn't get drafted. Instead, he went on to play for a team in Canada called the

Calvary Stampeders, and at the time, it paid him very little money. It got so bad for him that, at one point, he found himself dumpster-diving to get a mattress to sleep on. Then he got cut from that team and had to call his dad to come and pick him up. When his dad got to Calgary to pick him up, Dwayne remembers having seven bucks in his pocket. Actually he had six dollars and some change, but rounded up to seven bucks for the story. That's a back against the wall moment if there ever was one.

That is why his production company is called Seven Bucks Productions. He wants to always remind himself of how bad it got. He wants to remind himself to stay focused and hungry. He wants to remind himself how he found his grit. You are going to learn how to do the same. One last thing before we get started, we gotta talk about a few of the myths about grit that trip people up along the way. This is your mental warm up. Just like the physical warm-up always make sure that you prepare before you just jump in. One more mental stretch before we get into the meat and potatoes.

The Myths About Grit

This is the last prep part of the book before we get into the nitty gritty. Pun intended. We are breaking it all down like this so that you know everything that is coming at you on this next level of mental toughness! You need to know this stuff. It's a crazy world out there in these skreets. Plus, if I didn't tell you everything I know and how to avoid my mistakes, I would be doing you a disservice. So, here we go, the last session before we get into the how-to's.

Myth #1: Grit is a one-size-fits-all solution.

Listen, no matter what book you read, what talk you hear, what mentor you have or what program you take, you MUST always remember that there is NO one-size-fits-all solution for grit. There is no one-size-fits-all solution for anything in life, for that matter. Everyone who mentors you, including me, is going to tell you the steps that worked for them. Nine times out of ten, you are going to have to take those steps and add your own flavor for them to work for you. They will NOT work right out of the box. You are going to have do like Bruce Lee did and take what works for you out of what they teach you and discard the rest. Your grit will require your own special twist. So, take what I give you and use what works for you to make your own grit recipe.

Myth #1: Grit makes you less afraid.

Yeah, no. Grit doesn't make you less afraid. It just teaches you how to use your fear to move forward despite being afraid. Grit teaches you how to use fear to perform at your highest ability. Even the mighty Mike Tyson talks about how he used to be afraid before every match. Yeah, the guy who would knock heavy weight boxing champions out in the first round was afraid before **EVERY** match. However, he learned to use his fear to go from terrified boxer to champion in the short walk from the dressing room to the ring. That's what grit does. Grit helps you feel the fear and do it anyway. I put the video over on the download for you to hear him talk about it himself. It's pretty cool to see if you haven't seen it. Cus D'amato, his trainer, taught him this when he was only fifteen years old. In the video, Cus says this about fear:

"All people are afraid. Being afraid is a very normal, healthy thing. If an individual were not afraid, I would have to send them to a psychiatrist to find out what was wrong. Nature gave us fear in order to survive. And of course, fear is our best friend. Without fear, we would all die. We would do something foolish or stupid, which would cause our death or being crippled. Fear is something which has to be controlled."

– Cus D'Amato

So, no, grit doesn't make you less afraid. Grit teaches you how to control your fear and use it for your benefit. Be sure to check out that video of Mike Tyson talking about fear. It's a definite must-see. It was crazy for me to hear him say that he was afraid. It was great to hear how he harnessed his fear.

Myth #1: Grit makes you better.

Nope. Grit doesn't make you better. Getting better makes you better. Grit makes you more resilient. It makes you more willing to take chances. It makes you more determined to keep going, and as a result, you end up getting better results, which people will perceive as you being better. However, grit doesn't make you better. Working hard makes you better. Grit does, however, make you more persistent and more determined. I guess some will say having better results makes you better, and I see where they are coming from. However, as someone who is gaining grit as you read this book, you have to understand that the devil is in the details.

For instance, Babe Ruth had grit, and some people perceive him as the greatest homerun hitter of all time. However, and you may know this but, the year he won the homerun title, he also held the record for most strikeouts. So, based on the analytics, he was not the best homerun hitter. That's based on the number of swings and strikeouts. However, because he was willing to swing and miss, he had the most home runs that year. Yes, he had more homeruns than anyone else, but he also had more strikeouts. He was willing to fail 10 thousand times and because of it he held the homerun record for a long time!

Same goes for Michael Jordan's scoring title. As the NBA's fifth all-time leading scorer, MJ also held the record for most missed shots. Kobe came along and passed him with most points scored, becoming the fourth all-time scorer in NBA history, but he also passed him in most shots missed. You know who is the number one leading scorer in NBA history? It's the Legend Kareem Abdul-Jabbar. He also is top five in missed shots in NBA history. Does that make them better shooters than other NBA players? That is debatable. However, it does make them more willing to lose, and because they were willing to take more chances, more shots, more swings, they were able to have more success. That's grit.

Myth #1: Having grit will make you unbeatable.

Again, NOPE. Lots of people with grit lose. They lose a lot, actually! The difference is that they don't let the losses keep them down. They look at a loss as an opportunity to evaluate what went wrong and apply what they learned as a result of the loss so that the same mistake doesn't happen again. People with grit see their losses as an opportunity to grow. People without grit see loss as a permanent setback or some kind of judgment on who they are. Don't be like that. Have a growth mindset. Losses are just opportunities to grow and learn. Always think of them as that and only that. In an interview with Patrick Bet-David, Kobe was asked about his four air balls in a Laker's championship game.

Patrick reminded Kobe that in the moment Shaq pulled Kobe over and said some encouraging words to him. Patrick asked Kobe, "What did Shaq say to you in that moment?" Kobe answered, "I don't even know. I wasn't paying attention. For me, it's like…Maybe it was a little like asshole of me or whatever, but whatever. He was trying to whisper encouraging things, but I was like, 'I'm f%$#ing fine. Okay, I shot five air balls on national tv in front of millions of people that cost us the series, and I'm 18. I'm fine, dude.'"

In the video, he goes into grit mode like I talked to you about earlier. He explained how he looked at the situation after he had what many would consider a huge failure and kept going. Spoiler alert: He does exactly what I just told you people with grit do. Check it out for yourself on the download at mentaltoughnesspdf.com. You know the drill. The video is epic!

All right, now that we have gone through all the problemsand myths, and now that we have set you up for the main course of how to bring more grit into your life, let's get into the meat and potatoes of how you can make this happen in your life right now. Buckle up, buttercup. This is the fun part! First up on the grit agenda: eating frogs for breakfast!

CHAPTER 3

Frogs for Breakfast

"If you do what is easy, life will be hard. If you do what is hard,
life will be easy."

—Les Brown

(Player Perspective)

Welcome to How to Get More Grit: Step 1! First of all, notice that I didn't say, "How to scroll through your favorite social media before breakfast step 1." Yeah, that is a quick way to waste an hour or more of your prime brain processing time. Now, I'm not saying no social media at all. However, I am saying that doing anything on your phone first thing in the morning is wasting some of your strongest brain power performance time. The best way to get started developing your gritty self is to do the hardest thing you have on your list first thing every day: Eat your frogs for breakfast.

Now, I'm not actually talking about eating a real frog. So, for those of you who were ready to gross out your little brother or sister, y'all need to simma down now! It's basically a figure of speech. Mark Twain once said: "Eat a live frog first thing in the morning and nothing worse will happen to you the rest of the day." Basically, he means you should do your biggest or hardest task first thing in the morning when you wake up. In this chapter, you and I are going to look at the importance of doing the hardest stuff first. If you can commit to starting your day with your biggest, most difficult, ugliest task, you are going to have your second-degree mental toughness belt in no time.

Here's how the "eat the frog" method of developing grit started back in the day. Brian Tracy, a self-help author and speaker, read the Mark Twain quote and decided to try it out for himself. After he tried it out and liked the results, he probably shared it with his clients or something like that. Now, that is probably not the first time this was talked about or tried, but that's where my dad learned about it. I learned it from him so that's where we are going to start from.

Here's the deal, once your hardest task is out of your way, the rest of your day will feel like a breeze. Why's that? Because you now don't have that dreadful feeling of knowing that your really hard task is waiting for you at the end of your day.

What Is a Frog?

A frog is an important task that is going to take a lot of your time and/or energy. I know you all can figure out what your big tasks are, but I'm going to give you some qualifiers for frogs just so that we are thorough.

Frog Type #1 – The Important Task: Jumbo Frog

This frog type task is usually that one big task that you keep on the back burner because you are scared of making a mistake. You know you should do it. It's super important, but you keep putting it off until later. You might be scared that it will take all day. You might be sacred that you will do it wrong. Here's the deal. You're going to have to do it no matter what. Waiting to do it till later is not going to make it go away. It's not going to make it easier, and it won't change the outcome.

Eat the frog and do it first thing in the morning. Tackle important tasks head-on and let the chips fall where they may. Either way, you are going to be okay at the end of completing this type of task. How do I know? Because you have had this type of task before in your life, and at the end of the day, you always ended up okay. This one isn't going to be any different than the ten thousand other jumbo frogs you have had in your life. You are going to fine. Now get it done and let's move on.

Frog Type #1 – The Very Difficult Task: Big Frog

99.9% of all of the very difficult tasks are usually way more difficult in your mind than they are in real life. The difficult task monsters are usually much more frightening in your head. These "Big Frog" kinds of tasks are the types of tasks that you keep avoiding because you know it's going to be hard. Well, here's a pro tip: Waiting to do the difficult tasks isn't going to make it any easier. You're going to have to do it anyway, so just jump in. As you float downward towards the pool of cold, difficult task water, always remember one thing: Everything is always more difficult in your mind than it actually is in real life. Take on the monster. The closer you get, the more you will realize that the scary monster has no teeth. Because this scary task monster doesn't have any teeth. It's way harder in your mind than it is in real life. Just gotta do it!

Frog Type #1 – A Painful Task: Not-So-Big Frog

Muhammad Ali, he's one of the greatest heavyweight champs of all time—maybe even *the* greatest ever. When he was asked how many sit-ups he did in his workouts, Ali responded by saying, "I don't count my sit-ups. I only start counting when it starts hurting. When I feel pain, that's when I start counting because that's when it really counts."

Painful tasks just suck. There is no way around them. I can't really make it a feel-good type thing. So run right towards them. Be like the Rock, do you know what he says about his painful tasks? He says, "It's going to be so bad it's good!" That's next level grit right there. Challenge yourself and kick your painful tasks butt. Sorry, that's just what this one is. There is no easy way out. You may have some homework due soon. Maybe you need to do more research or something before you can get started. Maybe you have some bad news that you need to tell someone. Either way, this type of task comes with a lot of fear, dread and pain. Don't forget the pain part.

Know that it's going to suck. Know that it's going to be painful, but also know that after it's done, the rest of your day, week or month is going to be cake. Take a deep breath and get to doing. Like the Polar Bear Club, just jump in the ice water. It's not going anywhere, and after this, everything else is going to be easy! Win the day at the beginning of the day, and the rest of your day is a breeze.

Now That Frog Is on the Menu, How Do You Eat It?

I hope this isn't too basic for you, but I really want to make sure I go over everything step by step. Doing this "eating the frog first" thing is super important.

Eating your frog means you are going to have to form new habits. You are going to have to make a choice to choose hard every morning of every day. Even that in itself is a frog of a task, but, again, once you make that decision, the rest of your life gets a lot easier. Here are some of the things that work for me when it comes to getting the tough things done. You can steal any of them that you want.

1. Label your daily to-dos and put your frog at the top of the list.

Making a list is always great! As you know from the last book, writing things down is a great way to get your brain on board. Labeling your frog and putting it first on your list is more of a psychological win than anything else. Once you draw a line through that sucker, there is nothing like the relief that follows. Once you have the list of the tasks you want to achieve, use what is called the "ABCD Method" to put them in order even more.

"A" tasks are massively important. They are things you can't avoid. These are the things you gotta do. If there are too many of them, you can group them by adding numbers. For instance, you can write A-1, A-2, A-3, and so on. These are tasks that you have to do today and can't, or should I say, should not be skipped.

The "B" tasks are tasks that you *should* do. These types of tasks are worth doing, but your world won't end if you don't do them. For instance, say you need to clean your room. For the most part, if you clean your room, your room will look great, but it's not something that will change your life a lot if you do it tomorrow instead of today. That is, unless your parents told you to do it today or else. You get the idea. Basically, tasks in the "B" category aren't going to make much of an impact but might have some consequences if you don't.

The "C" tasks are nice-to-dos. These tasks have no consequences if they are not done. These tasks are things you just want to do because it feels nice. For instance, calling or texting to check up on a friend you've not heard from for a while or just calling your coach to check in.

The "D" tasks can be delegated to someone else since the "A" tasks will be taking up your time. You might be able to delegate them to get these tasks done. For instance, let's go back to mowing the lawn or shoveling the driveway. I brought up these examples because we all know an ambitious kid who has a lawn mowing or snow shoveling business. Heck, sometimes you can even pay your little brother or sister a couple of bucks to get them to do these tasks for you. If you can delegate the task and clear up more time, you should delegate "D" tasks and get more done.

The "E" tasks are unimportant things that should be eliminated. They might be fun—and we all know fun is great—but they're probably things you enjoy doing that don't have much value. Things like going to the mall, scrolling through social media or catching up on your favorite YouTuber. You get the idea.

Use this method of grouping tasks to evaluate your tasks regularly because priorities may change over time. Make sure that the way you prioritize your tasks is reflecting those changes.

2. Do what others don't.

Arnold Schwarzenegger said, *"Sleep faster"* when talking about how some people say they need eight hours. (Video over on the download.) The actor, retired bodybuilder and politician, encouraged waking up early by sleeping faster. What he was trying to say is there is no way around hard work if you want to win. You just have to face the hard work and do it. Waking up early allows you to get your hardest tasks done while everyone else is sleeping. I can tell you from experience that there is nothing like being done with all of your hard tasks before anybody wakes up. It's different. Your day looks wide open, and you feel amazing. Getting up early and tackling the hard tasks in the morning is definitely worth it.

Astrophysicist Neil deGrasse Tyson said, "There is very little in life that is worth achieving that isn't hard." According to him, if you are doing difficult stuff, you shouldn't dwell on why it's hard because that very fact proves it's worthwhile. Many people see tasks as tough because they can't do them, or should I say, choose not to do them. Even more people see things as tough because they don't want to do them. Doing hard stuff is, well, hard. But that's why you can name all the icons from your sport of choice on one hand, maybe two if you're lucky. If you think you can do it and go for it, you will accomplish more things than most people.

Retired wrestler and successful actor—and possibly future president—Dwayne Johnson, popularly known as "The Rock," hates doing cardio exercise. Do you know how I know? Because he does it first thing in the morning. Not just at 8 in the morning when everyone else is getting up. The Rock is running at four in the morning. He eats his frog at four in the morning. Everyone asks him how he does all of the things he does and how he's involved in so many things. The answer is what I am telling you right now. Go to bed early and get up early, and as soon as you get up, get to work eating your frogs. This success stuff is only hard if you try to fit your life inside the box of what is "normal". Normal actions get you normal results. The Rock works out twice and sometimes three times daily but makes sure he starts his day with cardio. That is his frog, so he gets it out of the way first thing in the morning—four o'clock in the morning.

Kobe Bean Bryant was a professional basketball player who prided himself in getting up early every day to focus on his training. He woke up at 4:30 am and was working out by 5 or 6 am. That is what he did to get started on preparing himself for his games and for his career. When asked how he was coping with his sleep patterns, Kobe said, "I don't need too many hours of sleep, man." Getting up early every morning wasn't just for basketball; he mentioned that practicing early gave him time to spend the rest of the day with his family.

Gritty people love doing the hard stuff first. If you win the day at the beginning of the day, the rest of the day is easy. Here is what science has to say about waking up early to do the hard stuff:

The New York Times had this to say about doing the hard things early in the morning:

- As humans, our willpower weakens throughout the day. As the day goes on, we face different situations that demand our attention. Focusing can be very daunting when trying to face the distractions.

- Tackling challenges first thing in the morning will help encourage the same behavior throughout the day. People who focus on doing hard things first are known to get things done more without procrastination.

Due to the brain's chemistry early in the morning, it's easier for you to be focused and fully alert first thing in the morning. You aren't overthinking in those early hours, and you can naturally do the difficult things you need to do for a great start. When you wake up, it's easier to absorb information. Make sure that you do the things that need your complete focus and attention during this time. Do the things that really matter in the morning, rather than rushing through your schedule to get to them later.

Will Smith says, "Where I excel is with a ridiculous, sickening work ethic. While the other guy's sleeping, I'm working." By getting up early, you will have time to get things done without distractions. Identify what your best ideas are and find the discipline that will make you do it, and find that discipline early in the morning.

3. Inch by inch, everything is a cinch.

Everyone loves the sense of completion, the feeling of reaching their goals successfully. However, when you are just starting, your goal is going to feel like it is way out of reach. So, break it down into smaller chunks. By doing this, you will have more manageable wins along the way. The small wins along the way help you stay motivated. Once you wake up early in the morning a bunch of days in a row and start putting your projects down on paper, you will see that one win always leads to another, which leads to another, which leads to another. After you complete the mini-goals, you can reward yourself for the efforts you've put in. The end of the task will become more and more reachable, and you will feel more and more confident that you can reach your goal with each small step.

Elon Musk once said, "Crazy things can come true. When I see a rocket lift off, I see a thousand things that could not work, and it's amazing when they do." Musk is one of those people who does things other people think of as impossible. He does so because he's more afraid of not trying than he is of failing.

Serena Williams, the tennis GOAT, says, "I work really hard. As long as you're willing to do hard work, you'll have everything." Serena is absolutely right because you will achieve anything you want if you push yourself hard. With dedication, the right mindset and hard work, there is nothing you can't achieve. By getting up early and winning the day every day, you get there a lot faster.

Alex Morgan, professional soccer player, had this to say about hard work: "Always work hard, never give up, and fight until the end because it's never really over until the whistle blows."

Author and speaker Gary Vaynerchuk says: "Not only am I working eighteen hours, I'm working fast as hell in this eighteen hours, and I'm prioritizing what's important and what's not."

You can't work 18 hours a day if you are sleeping eight. That's just not how 24 hours a day works. Either way, there are a couple things I want to make sure you get from this chapter:

- You are going to have to work hard to get what you want — probably a lot harder than you are right now. I can say that confidently because, right now, you don't have what you want. If what you are doing was enough to get what you want, you would already have what you want. Since you don't have what you want, clearly more work is necessary.

- You are going to have to decide to get up early. You are going to have to decide to win the day every day by giving yourself a chance at having more time. You are going to give yourself the gift of more time by getting up earlier.

Now it's up to you. Your move. Do you love sleep more than you love success or do you love success more than you love sleep?

Chapter Summary

- Tackle your frog (hardest task) first thing in the morning before you do other things.

- Frogs can either be the difficult, painful or important tasks. Sometimes they can be a combination of all three.

- Very few worthwhile things in life are easy. If you want to achieve success, you should be ready to push yourself a little.

- Make the decision to get up early and tackle your hardest tasks before everyone wakes up.

CHAPTER 4

Sacrifice to The Gods of Dreams

"There can be no progress, no achievement without sacrifice, and a man's worldly success will be in the measure that he sacrifices."

—James Allen

You Will Have to Offer a Sacrifice!

(Parent/Coach Perspective)

There is a price for greatness, and you must be willing to pay it. Dreams aren't easy to reach, but reaching them is super necessary. That's how gritty people look at their dreams. They are not only possible they are probable. Here's the catch. Dreams are not going to just fall into your lap. You are going to have to give up something to turn those dreams into reality.

Mitch Albom once said: "Sacrifice is a part of life. It's supposed to be. Sacrifice is not something to regret. It's something that you should aspire to."

Way too many people are looking for the easy road to success. Too many people don't want to experience pain or give up something for their goals and dreams. That's why companies make a killing selling millions, and in some cases billions, in training programs that promote products like "The 10-minute this" or "The 90-day that." Ask any trainer or any successful person what they think about those programs and prepare to hear the all-knowing chuckle. They laugh because they know that they didn't get the muscles they have by working out for only thirty minutes a day. They chuckle because they know that their success took much longer than 90 days. They got it from hours of work every day for a long time. In some cases, we are talking years.

This need to find the hack, or the shortcut is the major reason why dreams have remained out of reach for so many people. A lot of folks want their dreams on their own terms. They don't want to be uncomfortable. They don't want to spend too much money on training. They don't want to buy this course or that book. They don't want to spend that much time. They think that somehow, they should just be given access to opportunities. They don't want to invest in themselves more than what society will say is "reasonable."

Let me share something with you: Ninety percent of society isn't living their dream because they didn't go all-in on the sacrifice part of their dream-achieving journey. With that being the case, society might not be the best first stop on the "how to achieve your dreams" opinion-getting tour. Just sayin'. Here's the deal. You don't get to decide how much sacrifice your dream will take. Dreams come with their *own* terms of service and sacrifice requirements. If you want to be a dream-living person, you are going to need to believe in your dreams so much that you are willing to sacrifice whatever it takes to achieve them. Not gonna lie, that takes a lot of this thing called grit. It also takes a lot of sacrifice.

If you want to be successful in what you do, get familiar with doing things that aren't fun, easy or "realistic." Get used to channeling your energy into things that give you pain without immediate enjoyment or results. Sound brutal? Yeah, well... it is. To get where you want to be, you are going to have to make hard choices, and as far as your dreams and goals go, you are always going to have to sacrifice. There is no other way around it, my friend.

Actor Jennifer Lewis talks about how difficult her path has been coming from poverty to being a successful actor. She once told a story about being made fun of for having to go to the school out house to use the bathroom because her house didn't have one. I don't know about your life, but that sounds rough. She also said this:

"The elevator to success is broken—take the stairs."

Get up early and take the stairs. Achieving something great is going to require great sacrifice. I like to think of success as an energy exchange. You will NEVER get something for nothing. You will always reap what you sow. You will always get out what you put in. A lot of times that means you are going to have to miss out on temporary fun things in order to enjoy the amazing things that come with life-changing benefits in the future. Serial entrepreneur Gary Vaynerchuk had this to say when speaking about dreams requiring sacrifice:

"Dreams require sacrifices. People don't want to sacrifice because they are so used to mommy or daddy, or the system, or the government, or something else taking care of the bill part. You are entitled to dream, but not to your dream. You have to sacrifice."

As Dwayne the Rock Johnson puts on his t-shirts., **"RENT'S DUE!"**

If you can't make the needed sacrifices to achieve your own objectives and goals, you won't be getting them. There is nothing in life that isn't achievable. However, everything will stay just out of your reach if you aren't willing to sacrifice. Your sacrifice will be your money, your time, your energy and sometimes all three. Sometimes, you only need to sacrifice one of these, but that is pretty rare. Most of the time it's all of them.

If you want to achieve your goals, you are going to have to give up your comfort, pride, or what a lot of people call "a normal life". You can always determine the level of your likely success by the level of your sacrifice.

Things That You Might Have To Sacrifice

"Commitment is like... You almost have to give your happiness up to accomplish your goals," was Mike Tyson's answer when speaking with guest Eminem on an episode of his podcast "Hotboxin' with Mike Tyson."

Now to clarify, he didn't mean your happiness forever, Mike Tyson meant your happiness in the moment. Things like hanging out with friends or going to the mall and stuff like that. What he meant was that you are going to have to fall in love with delayed gratification. Mike Tyson and Eminem both have given up a lot to be where they are. How much are you willing to give for your dreams, goals and success? Your answer will let you know if you are ready to do the sacrificing required for your goals. No judgment. However, it is definitely something you should ask yourself. Move forward based on your answer. Now, let's take a look at some of those sacrifices I am talking about.

The Sacrifice of Sleep

Steve Harvey once said, "If you don't want to be uncomfortable, don't pursue success." Successful people often deliberately make do with less sleep. Those extra hours you stay awake to work can go a long way in pushing you towards your ultimate success. I mean, if you have eighteen hours to work on something while everyone else has ten to twelve, you definitely have an advantage. Without giving up the extra hours of sleep, you may not have enough time in your day to get all of the things done that you need to do in order to reach your goal. It's just math.

You saw what Kobe Bryant, Dwayne Johnson and Will Smith all said about waking up early to focus on a task. I mean, I could try to think of some cool way to spin it, but it really is that simple. More hours to work on your dreams means a higher likelihood of success. It also means less sleep. If you aren't willing to make the sacrifice for your goals do you really want to succeed?

The Sacrifice of Time

Olympian Michael Phelps was once interviewed about his training regimen. He went on to tell the interviewer what he did differently from other people. The interviewer on *Dubai Eye* was a little shocked by what he said but not too surprised. I am sure that they had heard this before and were probably using it in their life as well. I mean, you don't get to be an interviewer on a high-level show without understanding the sacrifice of time. Here is what the Gold medalist said:

"What I did wasn't rocket science. For me, as a kid, I had dreams bigger than anybody else ever dreamed… I wanted to be the greatest I wanted to be the best… and I always wanted to be the first Michael Phelps. Because I wanted to do things differently than everybody else. So for me when I went through a span of about 5-6 years where I didn't miss a single day of training 365 days a year that made me different.

I got 52 extra days each year than anybody else had. And…In the sport of swimming if you miss one day it takes two days to get back to where you were. So everybody else was taking a step back when they weren't swimming and I was taking that one step forward. So for me that's really all it was. I was willing to make sacrifices. The greats do things when they don't always want to and I think that's what separates good from great." – Michael Phelps

Sound familiar? I mean, that is pretty much exactly what Kobe said about how he became great. Everyone has access to the same twenty-four hours. We all have the same opportunity to use it effectively. By sacrificing your time for something, you are giving yourself an advantage. I know I said it before, but I wanted you to understand that this isn't rocket science. Sacrifice! Get up early and work hard. It's like giving yourself a head start every single day. When you do that, you automatically win the sacrifice of time game. Want to be the best? Give yourself more time.

The Personal Life Sacrifice

Don't get me wrong here, you shouldn't start thinking about how you are going to neglect your loved ones or disregard the people you love. That's not what I mean when I say this. However, what I am going to say is that if you are looking to be great, you may not have time for all the trips to your friend's house. You won't have time for all the activities regular people think are a requirement for a "balanced" life.

Hey, like I said earlier, if you want an exceptional life, you are going to have to sacrifice for it. Learn to say "no" to some invitations to parties and get-togethers. Like it or not, those things are distractions. You have to decide whether or not the cost of social time is worth you not reaching your goal. I didn't make up the rules, so don't get upset with me. Get upset with Michael Phelps. He said it first. You can see him say it over on the free download at mentaltoughnesspdf.com

Look, my friend, I'm just repeating what other greats have said. Sacrificing personal social outings and the like just seems to be part of the formula for success.

In one of his last interviews, Kobe Bryant revealed that he didn't have as much time for his personal life as he would have liked, but he saw it as normal because, as he said, other things will suffer when you are focused on succeeding. In his words, "The people that love you, like friends and family, know that about you. They let you be you, and when you reconvene, you pick back up where you left off." The people who truly love you will understand your sacrifices. Not only will they understand, they will support you.

The Delayed Gratification Sacrifice

As I tell my kids when we talk about them working on their goals while they are young, "You can go around the block on your bike today, or you can go around the world on your jet tomorrow."

I know we are a bit extra, but that's what it takes. At least that's what it takes for people like this.

- James Park, the creator of Fitbit, a 2.1 billion-dollar company recalls his mom telling him at 5 that he was going to go to Harvard.

- Richard Williams told his wife that he was going to have girls and they were going to be tennis stars before Venus and Serena were even born.

- LaVar Ball said that his sons were going to play in the NBA.

I guess that's just what over-achievers do. We call it like we want to see it in the future, and then we work to make it so. Look, being different is hard. There aren't a lot of people who do it, and that's why there aren't a lot of people who have achieved the goals we aim for. We all get tempted to choose easy options. I've done that countless times myself. It's normal to feel like you want things to be easier. I get it, but if you truly want what you are saying you want, you are going to have to learn the art of delayed gratification and hard work.

American physicist, futurist and professor, Michio Kaku, says that a young person's future success can be linked to how well they would do on the marshmallow test. What's the marshmallow test? It goes something like this. A certain group of young kids were asked..

Would you like one marshmallow now or two marshmallows in fifteen minutes?

Professor Kaku said that the kids who could understand that it is better to wait fifteen minutes to get two marshmallows were tracked and, more often than not, did better at life in the long run.

For instance, if right now you're thinking of ways to go on the internet and spend time on your favorite social media platform. You gotta understand that those platforms are designed to give you little dopamine hits as often as possible in order to keep you engaged and on the platform. The work is knowing the social media site will be there whenever you get done with the work you have to do. That direct message will be there. That email will be there. Whatever that little piece of electronic communication says is waiting for you, will be there. Your favorite YouTube channel or video isn't going anywhere. If you can wait to check your social media until after you've completed everything you needed to get done, you will find yourself in the group of the successful marshmallow test-takers.

"I wanted to be one of the best basketball players that ever played, and anything outside of that lane I didn't have time for."

—Kobe Bryant

There Are No Shortcuts

No matter how much you want to find the easy way to reach your goals, no matter how much you wish there were a quick option, my hope for you is that you realize a short cut doesn't exist. If it did, all the greats would be telling you about it. Since they are not, you can probably bet the farm that there isn't a shortcut to success.

Your success is determined by your willingness to manage your time. Your success is determined by your willingness to do what is hard. Your success is determined by your willingness to sacrifice. It's not a popular idea, but it's required doing if you want to be successful. Again, I didn't make the rules, I'm just sharing them with you. Don't go getting mad with me. I'm just the messenger. It's as simple as what all the greats who have gone before continue to tell you. Dominating in your sport begins and ends with sacrifice and hard work. It's one thing to know what it takes, it's another thing to actually do it.

Are you willing to make the necessary sacrifice? That is a question only you know the answer to. Your willingness to do the things you need to do will be a major contributor to the level of success you reach. Making small sacrifices equals small results. Huge success, on the other hand, tends to demand huge sacrifice. Which one are you willing to make?

Chapter Summary

- There is a price for every good thing you want to achieve.

- You can't avoid sacrificing some things for your greater goals.

- It is usually necessary to give up something to achieve success.

CHAPTER 5

Who Is Your Richard Williams?

"If you cannot see where you are going, ask someone who has been there before."

—J Loren Norris

(Player Perspective)

Having a great mentor will help you grow not only as an athlete but as a person. A mentor will push you to new heights as well as encourage you when times get tough. Who is your Richard Williams? If you don't have one, find one. How do you do that? Well, the first step is to get to work on yourself. The funny thing about finding a mentor is that mentors are usually looking for someone to mentor.

However, they aren't looking to just pick any random kid out of a crowd and start mentoring them. They want to make sure their advice is going to be put to good use. They want to make sure that their knowledge is going to be taken seriously. Mentors spend years, and oftentimes decades, gaining the information you are looking for. Sharing their years of experience with someone who isn't going to use it is a huge waste of time for them, and they know that.

So, if you don't have a mentor and you want to find one, get to work on your craft by yourself. Start now! Outwork your competition right now. Sacrifice your time, money and energy right now. Do all the things we already talked about in this book and your mentor will find you.

"When the student is ready, the teacher will appear."

—Buddha

In sports, there will always be highs and lows. In those times when things are not going your way, a mentor can offer some tips on what to do next. Mentors, coaches, trainers—no matter what you call them—can give you guidance on how to make the most out of your situation. They're there for you to vent to when things go wrong, and they are there to hold you accountable when you fall short of your own goals. Mentors will call you out when you are trying to find the easy way out and also tell you when you could use a little of that grit stuff you are reading about in this book.

Mentors play a huge role in the life of an athlete. Cristiano Ronaldo had Sir Alex Ferguson, his early coach. Cristiano says that he is the reason for all his success in the game of soccer. Ronaldo has gone on to win five Ballon d'Ors, and he's broken several football records. If not for his mentor, Uncle Toni, who brought him into the game and still mentors him to this day, you probably wouldn't have heard about the tennis champion Rafael Nadal.

You also have the Williams sisters, Serena and Venus of course. They have made a couple appearances in this book. Their father, Richard Williams, coached them when they were just little girls. It's unlikely they would have found their path or been as good as they have become without their dad behind them every step of the way.

To start with, it was he who introduced the game of tennis to them. I mean, the man decided they were going to be tennis players before they were even born. As he tells it, it all started after he saw the massive check being handed to a tennis player as a prize on TV. That day, Richard decided he was going to have daughters and raise them to be tennis pros. He taught his daughters to serve big and hit hard every time and everywhere on the court.

All throughout their early years in the game, Richard made most of the key decisions for Venus and Serena. It was him who decided that his girls shouldn't play in the junior tournaments. As a result of his mentorship, in October 1994, Venus—who was fourteen at the time—won her first professional match with hardly any junior matches under her belt. I'm sure there were people who criticized his decision not to have his girls compete in the junior category, but as their coach and mentor, he knew their development level. He knew what they were capable of. He was in a better position to decide for them. He knew when they'd be ready to play pro and he was right.

Even as tennis pros, Richard Williams still looked out for his superstar daughters. As their mentor, he still made a lot of decisions with and for them. As a mentor he knew what they needed, and he made sure that they got it. There was a stretch when Venus took time off from competing so she could study fashion. While people criticized her decision, he defended his daughter, saying that the world is bigger than just tennis, and that burnout can be just as challenging as a rival player on the other side of the court. That is some high-level mentoring right there. You need a mentor like that, and like I said earlier, you get one (if you don't already have one) by being the mentee they would love to have. See the earlier chapters if you are confused on how to do that.

So, who is *your* Richard Williams? If you are going to be successful, you are going to need one. Having someone who plans with you, pushes you and motivates you is super-important. I love the Richard Williams story. Did you know that when he began teaching his children tennis, he wrote a 78-page plan to turn his daughters into tennis stars? You just can't beat that! Find someone who wants the best for you so much that they are willing to write out a plan for your success. Find a mentor who will plan your success and help you go after your dreams all-in.

As we said earlier, a good mentor will not just improve your athletic life, they will also improve you as a person. Mr. Williams did not just teach his girls to be good tennis players. He, alongside his wife, Oracene Price, taught their girls to be confident, independent women.

How Your Mentor Should Sound

A mentor can be someone who has done what you want to do, or they can be someone who has shown others how to successfully do what you want to do. They can also be someone who is willing to learn what you need to do to succeed and go after it with you and for you when need be. Just because someone played the sport doesn't mean they are the best person to mentor you, and on the flip side, just because someone hasn't played the sport doesn't mean they can't guide you to greatness.

There is this silent assumption that legendary players will also have successful coaching careers. That is not always the case. I get why people think that, but like many old ideas on how to reach success, it just isn't true. You can teach what you know AND what you are willing to learn. Some of the greatest coaches were not great players. Some were not players at all. (See Bill Belichick). There are countless examples that fit this, and there are also examples of mentors who played and mentor really well. The baseline should be if their students or mentees have success. If so, you are in the right place. Here are the five major factors your future or current mentor should have.

1. They are honest with you.

This is the most important attribute you want to see in a mentor. A mentor should be that person who tells you the hard truth and not just what you want to hear. When the truth hurts, and it should hurt a little less when you know that it's coming from someone who cares about you. Remember, extreme honesty from your mentor will only help you get better. They are simply trying to get you to discover the best version of yourself as efficiently as possible. You can do whatever you dream. You just need someone who is not only going to make sure you understand how hard it's going to be but will also help you find ways to work through the roadblocks.

2. They defend you.

In the story above about Mr. Williams and his daughters, we see how he was always there to defend them against critics. His corrections came often and unlaced with all the sugar a lot of people are used to. I mean, the man moved his family to Compton so they could experience life with a little edge and then moved them to Florida so they could get better tennis coaching. So, even when you are at your lowest, your mentor should stand up for you while working to get you on your feet again. When you are at your highest, your mentor should be right there to celebrate for a minute or two, then follow it up with how you can be better. That's the way this thing goes. Long story short, find a mentor who defends you.

3. They push you.

A great mentor will systematically help you develop your grit. They will help you seek new, challenging tasks that can help you acquire new skills that you'll need in your sport. They will push you when you feel like you can't go any further and push you even higher when you reach your mountaintop. To a great mentor, the work is never done. There are levels, kid.

4. They are more passionate about the sport than you are.

When you work with a mentor who is more passionate about your sport than you are, it will rub off on you. You will see their passion in the way they talk about the sport. You will see it in how they envision the future, your future. In many cases, your mentor will be the one person who loves your journey more than you do. Cus D'amato once told a 15-year-old Mike Tyson that he would be champion of the world. Find a mentor who eats, sleeps and breathes your sport, then listen to them. One day, you will love it more than they do, but in the beginning, that might not be the case. In the beginning, your mentor might love your sport and your journey more than you. Why? Because they can see all the possibilities that lay ahead for you. That alone is exciting. Watch, learn and listen. Soon you will be taking their place in the "I love (fill in your sport)" category.

5. They are a great listener.

Your ideal mentor will listen more and talk less. Now, you might swear that all they do is talk, talk, talk, but that is only because they have so much information to share with you, and they know that time is limited. However, whenever they are in the company of other people who can influence your journey, watch them. They will become quiet. That's that gritty stalking thing we talked about earlier. They aren't quiet because they have nothing to say, they are quiet because they are listening and taking everything in. They are quiet because they are assessing, learning and sometimes stalking. To a mentor, everyone is prey. Everyone is competition, and everyone is either a resource or an adversary. They spend a lot of time trying to find out which one they are in the presence of. It's crucial that you always know.

Some young athletes will say, *"Well, I don't have any mentors."* However, in this day and age, you can start off by being virtually mentored by anyone you want. Thanks to the Internet, you can make contact with mentors all across the globe. The amazing thing about this is that you can hear from them whenever you feel like it, and if you watch them long enough, you will find that they will tell you the same things over and over again. You just have to do it! Listen to them! Here are some virtual mentors you can start listening to on YouTube right now:

- Richard Williams

- Warren Buffett

- Cus D'Amato

- Mike Tyson

- Les Brown

- Jim Rohn

- Oprah Winfrey

- Kobe Bryant

- Dwayne Johnson

- Diana Taurasi

- Sheryl Swoopes

- Serena Williams

To find out more about this subject, you really should get the free download on <u>mentaltoughnesspdf.com</u>. It's still free and filled with a lot of the additional material and videos I've talked about.

As we finish up this chapter, I'm going to say it again: Get a coach or mentor. They can serve as that extra morale booster, conscience criticizer, hard-nosed motivator and friend. They are the person you'll need in your corner to overcome the hurdles you will face on this journey. A few decades ago, it was more difficult to get a mentor, but in this digital era, your ideal mentor is just a few clicks away.

Chapter Summary

- You need a mentor because they can push you, defend you and help you plan your career.

- A good mentor should be one who knows the sport, is constantly learning about the sport, is passionate about it, remains honest with you and listens to you.

- A mentor need not be physically present all the time. Thanks to the Internet, you can have virtual mentors.

CHAPTER 6

The 1% Rule

"Success isn't overnight. It's when, every day, you get a little better than the day before. It all adds up."

—Dwayne "The Rock" Johnson

(Player Perspective)

Get 1% Better Every Day

Superhero capabilities are just around the corner. It's a long corner, but it's a pretty easy walk from where you are. All you have to do to get there is get one percent better every day. That's it. That's all you need. To develop your superhero mamba self, you just need to be disciplined enough to take small steps every day. A lot of people try to get one hundred percent better by tomorrow and that's a quick trip to Frustrationville. Champions know that this thing called super mental toughness is a marathon of small steps. They know the race isn't won today. It's won by taking small step after small step over years. Grit is being disciplined enough to be patient and consistent. Most people think grit is all about responding to severe situations. It's not. Grit and mental toughness are things that you do every day. It's a way of life, and the way you get better at it is by doing a little each day. You'd be surprised at how little you actually need to do to eventually dominate your sport.

Compounding Effect

It's a game of compounding "habit" interest. Pay more attention to the process of getting just a little better each day instead of focusing on the end result of being a lot better. There is something called a compounding effect that comes with the 1% rule. Right now, there may be people who are ahead of you. They can do this or that. They have physical traits that you don't have. It may seem like they are too far ahead to catch. But, if you get better every day by just 1%, that won't be the case for long.

Think about it this way: If you get 1% better every day, for a year, by the end of the year you will be 37x better than you are right now. Can you imagine what a different person you would be if you were 370% better than you are right now? Small steps are all it takes to get you there. Do the small things each day. The problem we have is that it also doesn't require much *not* to do it. There is a thin line between doing one percent of something and doing nothing. It's so small of a requirement that a lot of people think if they miss their goal of getting one percent better today, they'll just pick it up tomorrow. Then tomorrow turns into the next day and the next day and soon you are too far behind to benefit from the 1% a day process.

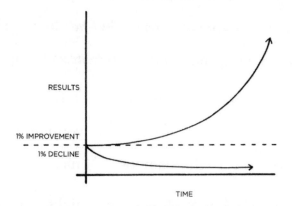

1% BETTER EVERY DAY

1% worse every day for one year. $0.99^{365} = 00.03$

1% better every day for one year. $1.01^{365} = 37.78$

FIGURE 1: The effects of small habits compound over time. For example, if you can get just 1 percent better each day, you'll end up with results that are nearly 37 times better after one year.

Taking small, consistent steps is the key to next-level success. Be the person who improves by 1% every day or end up being the person who gets a little bit worse every day. Like everything in life, there is no such thing as staying the same. Either you're getting better or you're getting worse.

Ask yourself: *Have I done anything today to improve by just 1 percent?* If the answer is no, get to it before you go to sleep. It really is that important.

Author and podcaster James Altucher says this about the 1% rule and getting better:

"There is a compounding effect that comes with improving a little every day. The 1% compounds and doubles every 72 days. The tiny excellence that has been compounded will then form a huge amount of excellence over time."

He went further by using math to show that 72 days of constant, tiny improvement will make you twice the person you are now in a very short amount of time.

If you get six hours of sleep per night, you will have eighteen hours of being awake to do something to improve. Now, multiply the eighteen hours by 60 minutes. That is

1080 minutes per day. 1% of 1080 minutes is 10.8 minutes. If you use 10 minutes every day to do something meaningful in your life, you can and will achieve something great over time.

Are your dreams worth 10 minutes a day? Would you be willing to spend ten minutes of your time focusing on getting 1% better? I hope you said yes because the greats are spending hours getting better. It really just depends on how much you want it and how much you are willing to invest in your bank of goals and dreams.

Habits and The Miracle of Compounding Interest

According to Albert Einstein, "Compound interest is the eighth wonder of the world. He who understands it, earns it; he who doesn't, pays it." The beautiful thing about compounding habits is that you can never run out of good habits. No one can take them away from you. Money is transactional; you can use it to buy something, and it's gone. Habits don't vanish when you use them. Using them will only make them stronger. That is why improving by 1% every day is huge for anyone who commits to it.

Creating good habits is one of the best things you could ever do for yourself. According to my extensive research (ha!), here's how you do it:

First, you need to define your goals, be specific about where you want to go, and what you want to be. Second, focus on getting a little better each time you go to the gym or step on the field. As you know from my first book, continuous practice is needed to improve the brain's myelin and boost growth and performance. If you don't have the book, go get it. It goes over a lot of stuff you need to know. It's called, *Mental Toughness for Young Athletes.*

Here's what James Clear, the famous author, has to say about tiny habits:

"Often, we have managed to convince ourselves that meaningful changes are only a result of large, visible efforts. Big changes are hard and unsustainable. Small steps add up. Take the small steps."

1% improvement isn't noticeable at first, but it will become very noticeable over time. Over time, the tiny improvements will compound, and you will suddenly realize that there is a huge gap between you and the rest of the pack.

"The key to realizing a dream is to focus not on success but significance, and then even the small steps and little victories along your path will take on greater meaning"

—Oprah Winfrey

Focus on the little things. Tiny, little habits and improvements are the key to your ultimate success. Sweat the small stuff. It leads to big results.

Chapter Summary

- The 1% rule requires that you improve by 1% each day. Follow this rule and you will eventually reach your goals.

- Habits are like money. When they are invested, they get compounded, stronger and make you richer.

- Self-improvement isn't achieved overnight. By taking small steps and constantly practicing, you will eventually be a better version of yourself.

CHAPTER 7

Talk Like Ali

"I'm not the greatest; I'm the double greatest. Not only do I knock
'em out, I pick the round."

—Muhammad Ali

(Parent/Coach Perspective)
Speak Your Reality into Existence

Now, before we get into this section, I am going to need for you to remember that you came here for help. This means that what you were doing wasn't working for you. So, you bought a book and started reading about some things that could help you do better. I'm going to need for you to continue to stay open to trying something new. Cool? Cool. Now that we have that out of the way, let's get started on this section.

On your journey to becoming the gritty mamba superstar in your chosen sport, there's something you need to learn and master. That thing is trash-talking. Yeah...I know... I know. A lot of people hate trash-talking. That's why I started this chapter off the way I did. Some people think it's unsportsmanlike, but that couldn't be further from the truth. The problem most people have with trash talking is that they think that it is about belittling the opponent. They think it's about tearing down someone else. That is not the purpose of trash-talking. At least, that is not why it was initially done. I'm kinda excited that I get to explain it to you because a lot of people get this wrong. I'm excited to be an ambassador for getting it right.

Let's get started. Those who use trash-talking the right way understand it the way that I'm about to share it with you. Trash-talking is basically an athlete's way of speaking their reality into existence. When Muhammad Ali "talked trash" about his opponents being slow or too ugly to be world champion, he was doing it to convince himself first that he deserved to beat them. He was convincing himself that they were beatable. When he said, "I'm going to knock him out in the fourth round," he was speaking the reality that he wanted to manifest into existence.

Listen, your words have power, and people who trash-talk understand that. Everything you say puts energy out into the world to make what you just said happen. A byproduct of Ali's trash-talking was that his opponents would worry about him fulfilling his prediction. They would often tense up, get nervous, or think about what he said during the fight as the round approached. During the round, they would make a mistake or leave an opening for the prophecy to be fulfilled. It is a whole subconscious mind thing. That's why you don't say things that you don't want to be true. Before you say it, ask yourself, "Do I want this to be true?" If the answer is "NO!" THEN DON'T SAY IT! I talked about it in the first book, but the long and short of it is that the subconscious mind can't hear the word *don't*. It just goes to work on whatever you say.

A command like, "Don't let him knock you out this round," is heard like this by the subconscious mind, "Let him knock you out this round." It's kind of crazy, but it's true. Ali was using every tool in the book to create his reality. The masterful use of trash-talking allows you to speak the reality you wish to see into existence. It has nothing to do with belittling the other person. Now that you know this, you must learn to use it too. I'm going to give you a peek into how the greats use it, and then you can make it work for you.

First off, don't think of it as insulting your rival. Think of it as a way to hype yourself up and convince yourself that you can do what you want to do. Think of it as speaking your reality into existence. You are saying the things you want to see yourself achieving. You are passionately convincing yourself that your goals are reachable. Think of it that way and only that way because that is the way that it's supposed to be done.

LaVar Ball spoke his reality into existence, and he did it in front of the world. A lot of people missed his genius because they didn't understand it. They didn't understand that his "trash-talking" was him speaking his reality into existence. He said his son would go number 1 in the NBA draft, and Lonzo ended up going number 2. Then he said he didn't think his son, LiAngelo, would play in the NBA, and he didn't play in the NBA. To this day, I don't know why he did, but that's the power of this stuff. He then followed it up with saying that his youngest son, LaMelo, would be his greatest basketball-playing son yet, and so far, he is proving that to be true. People hated him for doing this. Now they admire his sons for walking into the world that he spoke into existence for them.

Now for those of you who have haters or people who say that you can't make it. Let me tell you this. You can't make it. That is if you let their words become a part of your reality. You have to decide how it's going to be. You have to work insanely hard at your own goals and you have to believe. If there are people around you who don't believe in you, the align yourself with people who do. The main thing that you have to do is to work harder than everyone else. How do you do that? You take whatever you are doing and multiply it by 10.

Whatever workouts you are doing, you need to do ten times the work. For instance, if your goal is to make all of your free throws and you are shooting fifty a day shoot for five hundred. Whenever it's possible multiply your efforts by ten, and you might be getting close to what is required for you to succeed. Now let's get back to trash talking.

Again, trash talking is not supposed to be about belittling your opponent. That is not what trash talking is supposed to be about. Trash talking is simply meant as a use of one of our most powerful creation tools: our voice. The Bible says that God spoke the world into existence. That's how powerful your words are.

As a young athlete, I want you to start changing the way you see trash-talking. See it as passionate affirmations for success used by people with grit. Gritty people use trash-talk to motivate themselves. They use trash-talk to speak their desired reality into existence. They use trash-talk as a way to tell their subconscious mind what to create.

Don't feel comfortable saying it out loud? Say it in your mind. I got that from the audiobook "Maverick Mindset" by Dr. Jon Elliot. It's a great book. If you can find a copy definitely get one. I think that they are out of print so good luck. Whether you say your trash talking in your head or out loud, you are going to need to do it if you want to be like the greats. Doing it internally means you will tell yourself those words of affirmation that can boost your confidence inside your head. On the other hand, you can also choose to shout them out as loudly as the great Muhammad Ali. Either way, start doing it NOW! You are creating the world and the outcomes you want to see.

Ali wasn't the only one who trash-talked. Greats such as Michael Jordan, Kobe Bryant, Larry Bird, Babe Ruth, Steph Curry, Derek Jeter and Charles Barkley all took pride in trash-talking. Old-time athletes like Babe Ruth and Satchel Paige—and probably thousands before them—did the same thing. I actually put a video of professional baseball players talking about why they trash-talk on the free download. Go get the download, see what they say, then come back here. Ya welcome! Go to <u>mentaltoughnesspdf.com</u>. It's still free!

Did you know that Muhammad Ali was a quiet kid and didn't really use trash talking that much. That changed one day when he saw a wrestler by the name of Gorgeous George. Can you believe The Great Ali got his trash-talking lessons from watching a pro wrestler ?

Before seeing the wrestler, he used to do all of his trash talking in his head. Then he saw how the crowd was responding to Gorgeous George. Ali said he saw how the crowds responded to George and thought, *I want to be like that.* He got the crowd's attention with this and probably sold a lot of tickets. His trash-talking was a way to speak his reality into existence and fill seats. There is a video of him talking about it over on the download as well. At no time does he say that he trash-talked to tear down his opponent.

"Float like a butterfly, sting like a bee. George can't hit what his eyes can't see. Now you see me, now you don't. He thinks he will, but I know he won't. They tell me, 'George is good,' but I'm twice as nice. And I'm gonna stick to his butt like white on rice."

In another interview, Ali told the reporter the reason he was successful was because he thought differently and acted with confidence. Ali once said, "I wrestled lightning. Thrown thunder in jail." Now, we all know he didn't really do any of that, but that kind of trash-talking was great for psyching himself up—and for selling tickets. I'll say it again: Trash-talk isn't about your opponent. It's for you and your mental confidence, and in some cases, selling tickets. You're probably not selling tickets yet, so use it to build your confidence.

Before his fight with George Foreman, Ali named George "The Mummy." When asked why he called George "The Mummy," he stood up and mimicked George's movement around the ring. He talked about how slow and easy to avoid he was. He did it in a ridiculous way, and the interviewer and the audience couldn't stop laughing. However, the real reason he did it was to, one, be like Gorgeous George and fill the arena, and two, to build up his own confidence.

For those of you who don't know, at the time, George Foreman was undefeated. Foreman was seen as invincible. George Foreman was seen as one of the most powerful punchers in heavyweight history. He had easily destroyed top fighters like Frazier and Ken Norton—men who had given Ali tough, close fights. Plus, he was younger than Ali. Ali needed to convince himself that he had a chance despite Foreman being younger, stronger and having knocked out opponents whom Ali had struggled with. He had to convince himself that he had the tools to win and that Foreman was beatable. So, he kept speaking it into existence. After all, it had worked once before.

"He's Too Ugly to Be World Champion."

This is what Ali said in 1964 before his title fight against Sonny Liston. At the time, Liston was viewed as the scariest heavyweight champion ever because of his toughness and ferocious punching power. Sound familiar? But Ali acted as though Liston was going to be an easy fight. He made it seem like he was a hero who was going to save mankind from a monster. I mean, what would you do if you were facing someone who was not only knocking other boxers out but knocking them across the ring like Sony Liston did?

What's funny is, now that you know this, I want you to take a look at Ali at the end of the first fight. If you are paying attention, you will see that he is just as shocked as everyone else that he won. Young Ali knew the power of his words, but I believe that, up until that moment, he only believed it in practice. Up until that moment, it was something that was more academic, as they say. Then when it actually happened, everything changed. Take a look at the video of him after the fight on the download and tell me that man wasn't just as shocked as everyone else. That's the power of the spoken word.

Ali is one of the greatest of all time in the sport of boxing because he worked on both his physical strength and his mental strength. Trash-talking was a part of that mental work. Just imagine the mental picture he painted with his words inside his mind. That's the real advantage of all this stuff.

Before we wrap this up and you get to talking trash any kind of way, let's go over a few ground rules.

Unwritten Rules of Trash-Talking

First and foremost, you have to remember that whatever happens on the court or field stays on the court or field. If someone trash-talks you, it has everything to do with the game and nothing to do with you personally. I can't say that enough. Don't take trash-talk personally. Get over this whole "disrespectful" thing. First of all, you guys are teenagers or preteens. You aren't really owed respect as an athlete yet. You haven't done anything to earn it! Your parents have, your coaches have, but you are just a kid. As Kobe said, "Get over yourself." Understand where you are in the process.

I know I have said this a lot, but I want to make sure I drive this point home: **Trash-talking is a way of verbally competing in the game or competition. It is not a personal attack on who you are as a person. It's not meant to put down or disrespect your opponent. It's a mental tool to build up the trash-talker's own mental confidence.** Always remember that and stop thinking you are entitled to some fake level of respect. Get over yourself.

Don't make an enemy out of someone who is being verbally competitive. They are just being competitive. Remember, they are not doing this to attack you personally, and if they are, feel comfort in knowing that they don't know how trash-talk is supposed to be used. That means that they're probably all in their feelings. People who are in their feelings are very easily defeated. Welcome to your second-degree mental toughness black belt, my friend. Stay out ya feelings.

This is all about understanding the tool you have and how to use it. I'm going to give you a little trick that most people seem to miss more often than not. People who use this technique the right way and see that you are not fazed by their trash-talking will gain respect for you. Game recognize game. That's why Michael Jordan loved Kobe so much. Kobe would not only talk back, but he would back it up. They both admired each other because they knew the other understood what trash-talking was really for. See the video about Kobe and Mike trash-talking and going after each other on the download. They also talk about the going silent thing that gritty players do. You gotta check it out.

Jordan recognized that Kobe was one of his tribe. Samurai respect and honor other samurai when they see them. That doesn't mean they don't go after them though. In Jordan's words: "This trash-talker knows that my trash talk is for me and not about him, so he combats my trash-talk with his own. It's not a personal attack, so I don't have to get emotional. I just have to respond with my own trash-talk or confidence-building affirmations."

As Stephen Curry put it, "Trash-talking is a part of the game. You have to give it. You have to be able to take it. It's just that you don't want to see it ever cross the line and become personal because the game of basketball is never that serious in regards to disrespecting people. So, you have to leave it on the floor."

If you allow yourself to take trash-talking away from the field, court or pitch, you are breaking the rules of trash-talking. It's really that simple. It's part of the game so you leave it in the game. That is, if you are doing it right. According to Tyronn Lue, most young athletes wouldn't have survived the 1980s and 1990s. He said that any athlete who takes trash-talking seriously wouldn't have been able to play the likes of Gary Payton, Reggie Miller and Larry Bird. According to him, those greats talked trash like it was their job. They understood that it was just part of the game. Now you do too.

I just gave you a tool that most of your peers don't know how to use. If you catch people talking trash and getting all in their feelings then smile and nod because you know what trash talking is for—guess who has the advantage. YOU! Use it! As the story goes...

There was a game when Kobe was being guarded by Tony Allen of the Memphis Grizzlies. Tony says that he was guarding Kobe and Kobe was scoring on him and muttering a bunch of dates. Tony said that, later, he went back and looked them up, and they were the birthdays of all of Tony Allen's cousins. That is some next-level trash-talk from someone who understands the purpose of trash-talk. It's the game within the game.

Trash talking is not a thing of the past. We still have a lot of trash-talkers scattered across different sports. A notable example is José Mourinho, the head coach of the Tottenham Hotspur football team. Mourinho has won several trophies across different continents with different teams. He's also well-known for his trash-talking antics. At one point in his career, he said he was "The Special One." It was pretty much verbal conformation of what he had accomplished. He was telling his subconscious mind that it had done what it was supposed to do. (Check out the Video on the download). Another example is Draymond Green of the Golden State Warriors. That guy is the most candid and most amazing trash-talker I have seen in a while. "Dat boi gooood!" He is definitely the Dennis Rodman of his era. He talked trash to Marc Gasol while motivating his teammate James Wiseman. There are levels to this thing. He was basically building up his teammate in front of his opponent.

Then there is Dwayne "The Rock" Johnson, who was voted as the number-one trash-talker in wrestling history. When he was wrestling, he didn't care who he talked about. He didn't just go after opponents. He went after fans, reporters and anyone who he felt was standing in his way. His trash-talking made him one of the most popular wrestlers of all time. Like Gorgeous George he was using it to fill the seats. This is working so well for him that he is thinking about running for president. How amazing is that!

If you want to get used to the trash-talking game, check out the videos and supplementary materials over at mentaltoughnesspdf.com. Just as long as you don't forget to improve your abilities in the sport while you're upping your trash talking game. Trash-talking is cool, and it can be effective, but make sure your verbal affirmations can be backed by action when the time comes!

Chapter Summary

- Trash-talking is good because it helps you boost your confidence. It's not meant to spite your opponent.

- Trash-talking is effective because a key component of sport is the mental aspect. When an athlete is in the right frame of mind, they perform better.

- It's not enough to know *how* to trash-talk. You must also remember that there are rules, and you have to know how to take it without allowing it to ruin your game!

- Realize that trash-talk is not your opponent's way of saying they hate you. They are doing it for themselves, so don't take it off the field.

CHAPTER 8

History 101

"When you are not practicing, someone else is getting better."

—Allen Iverson

(Player Perspective)

Practice. Yes, we are talking about practice...and history. I bet you didn't know Allen Iverson said that quote about practice, did you? Every sport has a history. Before you started playing your sport, a lot of other people did what you are trying to do. Some of them were successful; some of them failed. Knowing your history can help you learn from the experiences of the greats and not-so-greats of the past. Knowing the past will help you win now and in the future. Why? Because most young athletes don't know their history. Most young athletes are trying to be the "new, never seen before, never been done before" original. Most young athletes don't take tips from greats like Pele, Kobe, Venus

Williams and others did. Greats are people who study past greats and add their techniques to their game. Knowing your history gives you an advantage. Take the advantage and start learning the history of your sport.

Let me put it to you this way, Kobe Bryant studied Michael Jordan and pretty much copied him. Now pay attention to what I am about to tell you. Despite there being a lot of film on Jordan showing how teams beat him, apparently nobody watched it and applied it when Kobe was in the NBA. You know what basically happened? Kobe stole Jordan's moves and used them 10 years later, and still dominated the NBA. He beat the players and teams in the NBA with old Jordan moves. How crazy is that!

Study your sport! Know its history. You can read books and watch old documentaries on YouTube and ESPN. You can visit sports museums, and have older athletes tell you some of their stories, but knowing your history is a game-changer. Nick Foles said this about studying the old game film: "There's a lot of it. Of course, every morning, we meet early and go to our quarterback's room, and that's what we do—we watch films. We look for things. And then we have meetings when we aren't practicing, and we watch more. It's a lot, I know that. It takes up so much of the day."

Watching current and old film is an awesome tool for developing your grit and knowing your history as a player. If you are watching film already, my advice is that you do it more often. If you haven't, the time to start is now. There is a video (on the download) of Ed Reed and Ray Lewis talking about how much they devoured film in their career. These guys are Hall of Famers. The greats are often the people who took the time to understand the history of their sport, and then reaped the rewards as a result.

You're probably thinking, *I know film study can improve my game because I get to copy the skills I see the pros exhibit, but how exactly does it improve my grit?* I like to think about it this way: When you were a baby, every day, you watched live film of people walking and talking. All day, every day, you watched the adults around you walk around without even thinking about it. You watched them have conversations with ease. Your brain was fed "how-to" information on walking and talking twenty-four hours a day, seven days a week. Because of the live film that you watched all day every day, now you walk around without even thinking about it.

If someone were to challenge you and bet that you couldn't walk across the floor right now, you would probably call that bet, and because you have watched film, you would win that bet. That is grit. You already have grit in life, you just need to apply that same work level to your sport.

Practice like a baby, and your gritty mastery is just around the corner.

That one sentence right there was worth the price of this book. Remember that knowing the history of your sport isn't confined to watching old games of your favorite old-timers. It also involves knowing the history of these old-timers. Some of them achieved their greatness despite very difficult situations.

It's a lot easier for you to be great when you know that someone did exactly what you want to do when they were in an even worse situation. It's a lot easier to know that you can score like Kobe when you realize that he is one of the NBA's top scorers, but he also leads in missed shots! It's a lot easier to chase Babe Ruth's home run record when you realize that he also had the most strikeouts the season in which he had the most home runs. How are you going to know these things if you don't know the history of your game? You aren't. You have to study.

A lot of the time, young athletes only see the wins and the makes. Knowing your history will help you understand the whole situation. Knowing your history helps you relax and go after your goals with grit and determination. Knowing your history helps you see the failures behind the shiny records that flood the social media airways. Knowing your history helps you understand that there are often some less-flattering numbers and statistics behind the reported amazing feats. Knowing all of this stuff will help you keep going when you have that not-so-good run, or game, or whatever.

A lot of young players will get upset when they only score four or five points in a basketball game or have a low batting average. The funny, not-so-funny part about it is that they often only take a few shots, or they don't swing their bat for fear that they might strike out. The guys you see with the scoring titles are taking eight shots a quarter, and a lot of times, more than that. The guys with a lot of hits also have a lot of swings and a lot of misses. You can't miss them all! You are putting yourself up against odds they couldn't even reach if you don't take chances. Study your history, watch films of games, and you will be amazed at how you just become naturally gritty.

Watch Your Own Game Film!
Watch Yourself Play.

As time goes on, you should start having your games recorded. Don't just watch other players play, start watching yourself play games too. You can use this game film to catch your own errors in the game. Watching yourself play will allow you to see what you need to work on. It will help you figure out how you can avoid the mistakes you're making in your game. For instance, a football player can use film of a game to check if team members are in the right positions during the game. It's one thing to tell your teammate to make sure they don't miss their assignment, but being able to lay out in detail how they tend to miss their assignment and how they can fix it, because you have watched the game film, is next-level.

It might not be easy for your coach to do this while the game is going on because there are, in some cases, 22 players plus the referee running all over the place. Sprinkle in heightened emotions, and voila, you have a brain overload. That is, if you haven't watched film. Game film offers a second chance for a proper look at what is going on. When you are away from the situation, you can really think about how you can fix it for the next time.

Watch your game film with your mentor or coach. You can scrutinize it together. Your coach or mentor can point out mistakes and the possible ways to keep them from happening again. However, don't forget to talk about the great plays you made too. Your subconscious mind needs the reinforcement every chance you get.

Watch Your Opponent Play.

Lebron James is a master at this. I put up a couple videos about players talking about him knowing where they were going to be and where they were supposed to go on the download. That is playing the game at mastery level, and it's really as easy as watching game film. Use game film to study your opponent before games. Get film of your opponents' games and study them. With the information you can get from watching their game film, you can make your plans and have them at the back of your mind while practicing. Study your opponent and you are going to be surprised at how easy it will be to predict how they will react. When you watch game film, it's like re-watching your favorite YouTube video. You already know where the funny parts are. With that in mind, you can come up with a strategy for the game and for your opponent. The big teams you know and admire use this tool in preparation for most of their matches. Start doing it now and you will be way ahead of your peers.

To get the best out of watching game film, make sure you write down a paragraph or two for all your observations. Knowing you are going to need to jot something down at some point during your film-watching session will help you watch film better in the future and get the most out of it. This reminds me of a story that Chicago Bulls player Patrick Williams tells about being on the floor with NBA great Lebron James in one of the videos on the download. As the story goes, during the game, Lebron was calling out Bulls plays before they even happened. He was even telling the Bulls players when they were in the wrong spot for a play. That's how you study film. That's a next-level flex. To watch so much game film that you know what the coach is going to call based on the situation is mastery-level stuff.

Film Study Boosts Confidence

Confidence is essential in any sport, and film study will give you that confidence. As you watch your favorite athlete play and achieve incredible things, you become aware that it is possible to do those things too. Basically, if they can do it, you can do it too. Without you realizing it, your subconscious mind will be picking up their signature moves, and when you are in training, you will see yourself attempting them. You will find yourself on your Kobe-type thing, going through great players' moves like they were originally yours.

Research by the University of Montreal shows that watching videos of athletes can improve your game. According to their research, you can improve your motor skills just by watching someone, which makes sense because that's what you did when you were learning how to walk when you were a baby. We talked about this in the first book, so you should already know this, but watching a professional performing a skill at a high level will help you do the same. I know it sounds crazy, but it's true. It's called the engraving technique, if you haven't read the first book.

Study to Show Thyself Approved

According to Chris Paul, watching film is a way of studying and learning not just players' tendencies but how they play their games. The NBA veteran talked about film study and how knowing the history of your game can give you that extra edge. In an interview, Chris Paul talks about how he is always watching game film. He says he usually has two or three games on at the same time. He credits his ability to see the floor with his constant watching of game film. I'm telling y'all, this is a cheat you need to start using now! Video over on the download!

In another clip (*over on the download of fire*), the boxing coach, Cus D'Amato, tells of the benefits of watching old fighters. He gave an instance of Floyd Patterson, who, he said, read all his books and magazines on boxing to the extent that he knew more about previous champions than Cus himself did. Cus said that indicated the young boxer's passion and drive, and it all paid off. Floyd became heavyweight champion of the world in 1956.

In the video, Cus and Mike Tyson go over a fight on TV and analyze it. Cus, being a mentor, answered some of the questions Mike had. This brings me to another big part of film study. It is more effective when done with a mentor who knows the game, but if you don't have one, just watching more film will improve your game. Mentors can point out things you probably wouldn't have noticed on your own. So, if you have a mentor already, great! It is time to go over some games and have them analyze them with you. It can make you a better athlete, just like it did with Mike.

Also, your film watching will be more effective if you are watching clips of people you admire. Of course, we all have the legends we like, admire and hope to be like one day. That's a given. But now you know that you can become more like them by watching their film. Science has shown that you will subconsciously replicate the behaviors you observe in the people you admire. This automatically happens when you watch a lot of game film.

This isn't just true for sports. Everyone who is anyone great at what they do will study the greats of the past. You probably haven't heard of the Rolling Stones and the Beatles, but your parents have. Both of those bands studied blues music greats when they were getting started. Then they put influences of the blues musicians into their own music. It seems this curiosity and need to know more is one ingredient for success. Most of the greats have indulged in it at one point in their career or another. You should do it too if you want the great results that come along with this stuff. Knowing your history helps improve your future.

Last but not least, don't limit yourself to people in your sport. The truth is, winners everywhere have similar habits. They are dedicated people who share the same determination and attitude in achieving their dreams. You will be doing yourself a huge favor if you take a page out of their book. Study people outside of your sport. Find out what they do and did to become great. Ask yourself how you can apply their skill to what you want to do.

Watch live games whenever you can, especially if someone who is considered a great in your sport is playing. Commit to really knowing your sport and your sport's history. Knowing your sport's history develops your IQ in the game. You will find yourself automatically getting better at all aspects of the game. The game will slow down and get super easy the more you watch. You will also know that nothing is impossible because many other people have achieved what you are trying to achieve—and many of them probably had fewer resources at their disposal than you have.

Chapter Summary

- Know the history of your sport; it challenges you to achieve impressive heights just like others before you.

- A key route to knowing the history of your sport is watching game film. This can help you learn new plays, identify the mistakes in your own approach and analyze an opponent before a match-up.

- Use online resources to read and watch all you can about your chosen sport and its major players.

CHAPTER 9

Copy Like Kobe

"Good artists borrow. Great artists steal!"

Pablo Picasso

(Player Perspective)

Everybody wants to be unique. Somewhere, somehow, someone convinced us all that it was great to be the "original, one-of-a-kind, never seen before" type of person or athlete. However, you can't name one great person who didn't take from others to enhance their own greatness. Trying to start from scratch and build your own never seen before person or athlete is dumb and a waste of time. Want to know why? Because, despite everyone saying there is only one you—which is true—there is also only one Planet Earth and one human race, which means that the same problems and same solutions have been around for thousands of years at minimum. That means that the only thing new is the fact that *you* haven't encountered the problem before. That means your experience of the situation is new, but the actual situation is old as heck!

That's why learning your history is so important. That's also why copying like Kobe works so well. Somebody has already solved the problems you are trying to solve. Learn about them. Learn from their mistakes and apply the information they have learned to your situation so you don't have to go through what they went through. Your goal should be to start where they left off, not where they started. However, that is not what most people do. Most people are still trying to be that original gangsta athlete, which doesn't exist. Don't do that! We have come to erroneously believe that if we copy or admit that we copied someone else, then it means we are not smart or sufficient enough to do it on our own. We think it makes us less creative or inventive than the person we copied.

Well, that is freakin' ridiculous. What if I told you that copying is a skill you need to survive, and it is actually super healthy? Going back to my earlier example, think about how babies copy the actions they see people do around them until they grow and become adults. Imagine if every baby was like, "You know what, I'm going to start my own language. I'm going to be an individual original. I'm going to be a one-of-a-kind." Imagine if everyone said, "I'm going to develop my own way of adding one plus one," or "I'm going to make my own way of driving a car." The list goes on and on. We would be a societal mess. (See common core math. HA!) However, that is not what we do with the things our lives depend on. Instead, we see what has been done, and if we are feeling ambitious, we add our own flare to what has already been successful. Not when it comes to sports.

In sports, we try to start from scratch, and that is super dumb! Don't do that! Learn what worked and then add your special sauce to it. Don't just skip to the special sauce part without the history and fundamentals. Nobody you know of came out of nowhere and suddenly achieved greatness. They all stole from someone else. All of those one-of-a-kind greats you look up to, read about, and learned from those who have gone before. They all steal from and mimic other athletes' work. You don't have to recreate the wheel. Someone already made a wheel, and it works great. Your only job is to put your own rims on it. When you do, that will be all you need to start working towards your G.O.A.T. status. Keep it simple!

Can you imagine trying to learn how to play golf without ever having watched someone take a swing? If you want to be a professional golfer, you have to study golf greats like Tiger Woods and see how it's done. From there, you can start to add your own creativity and personality into your game. This is the reason people have coaches and mentors. What they are doing is simply showing you how people before you succeeded. When you make those runs, jumps, and throws, you are directly or indirectly mimicking people who have done it successfully before you.

Why It Is Easier to Copy Than Not
It's Human Nature

Think of how you learned pretty much all the basic human activities you do today without thinking about them. You learned them by observing other people in your environment. That is what everyone does. Did you know that some of these activities you and everyone else learned to do easily are really hard things to do? Learning how to talk is a pretty hard thing to do. Don't believe me? Try doing it right now with a different language. Walking on two feet is a pretty hard thing to do. Don't believe me? Try learning how to walk on your hands as easily and as often as you do on your feet. We learn by copying experts. Our parents and guardians are really good at speaking the language we speak, so we copy them. They are really good at walking around, so we learn from them. That's often why people will say things like, "Wow, you sound so much like your mom or dad."

This is the power of copying the people around you. All humans learned these basic activities because they were exposed to them long enough. There's a saying that goes: "Show me your friends, and I will tell you who you are." By being exposed to people, you start acting like them, even without intending to.

As a young athlete, use this to your advantage. Expose yourself to other people who have succeeded, and you will see yourself succeeding like them.

Every Problem You Have Has Already Been Solved by Someone Else

Copy those who have succeeded before, and you will reach their success, or at least close to it. Why? Because most problems are the same old problems that other people have already solved. If you choose to start your own problem-solving mission without looking at what other people have done in your field, you will make several mistakes before getting it right—that's if you ever get it right.

By copying others, you are putting yourself in position to learn from their mistakes. Start where they left off. The fact that they are adopting a particular approach should tell you the other alternatives didn't work, or they weren't as effective as the way they chose. Learn from what they did wrong and at least don't do that. Look, you are still going to get things wrong. Just don't allow yourself to get the same problems wrong that someone has already solved.

Greats Who Copied Others and Excelled

In one interview where Michael Jordan was asked who he would like to go up against if he were in his prime. He said that the only one that he might lose against is Kobe because Kobe stole all his moves! If you have watched both men play, you will see exactly what he was talking about. Kobe didn't try to deny the fact that he copied Jordan. In a piece published in Bleacher Reports, he stated that the comparison was correct. It wasn't just basketball moves that Kobe copied. He also copied Jordan's mannerisms, ideology and ruthlessness.

Devin Booker from the Phoenix Suns did the same thing; he copied Kobe. Here is a comment from Kobe himself when he was talking about Devin Booker on a game where they played each other. Devin stole his move, the move he stole from Jordan, and Kobe recognized it. The move was a pivot fadeaway jump shot. Here's what he said,

"It was a carbon copy of my stop-pivot-turn-fade, which I learned from Michael." He went on to say how much of what he did was learned from Michael, *"Damn near 100 percent of the technique, damn near 100 percent."* Kobe picked up the

technique from Jordan and made it his own. Then, a younger player, Devin Booker, picked it up from Kobe, and someday, someone will copy it from Devin... I hope.

As we all know, Jordan and Kobe ended up facing each other a few times in their careers. It was in those moments that Kobe learned things straight from his mentor while playing the game. That had to be surreal. In one interview, Jordan talked about how Kobe came to him after a game and asked him about how he turned around when performing a jump shot. Kobe was relentless. However, the carbon copy got the same results as the original.

Kobe Bryant went on to break some of Jordan's outstanding personal records. One of them was the most field goal attempts in the history of the All-Star Game. Another one was the most total points in NBA All-Star Game History—Kobe had 265 combined points compared to Jordan's 262 combined points. That's what you can achieve when you copy winning formulas from those who came before you. Kobe was always very vocal in his admiration of the great Jordan, and Jordan loved that he had a worthy mentee to give all of his knowledge to.

Other Greats Who Copied:

- Muhammad Ali studied a lot of boxing greats and pulled a little from each one. He copied and made a new character out of all of the bits and pieces he put together. Muhammad talked about copying a little from Joe Louis and a little from Sugar Ray Robinson. He also took a little inspiration from a wrestler named Gorgeous George like we talked about earlier.

- Mark McGuire studied and copied Babe Ruth.

- Wayne Gretzky studied and looked up to Gordy Howe.

- Bruce Lee did like Muhammad Ali. He studied all forms of martial arts constantly. Taking what he thought was useful from boxing, wrestling and Chinese and Japanese martial arts, he developed his free-form method, which he called Jeet-Kune-Do.

- Jason Williams talked about watching Pistol Pete Maravich and picking up skills. He'd look at old black and white footage to try and pick up some of his techniques. He said that if he saw something he liked, he would go straight to his room or the gym and practice it until he made it his own.

- Serena Williams was a copycat too. Serena copied her older sister Venus. When they first started playing tennis, Venus, being a bit older, had a more powerful and dominant serve than Serena. Serena admired Venus and wanted to do everything her older sister did, so she developed her game and added more power to her shots. Later in life, she could even beat Venus.

These are just a few examples of notable athletes that copied others. The truth is, most—if not all—athletes look up to people and learn how they went about their work. Do what they did. It works! Got a video of them talking about copying too.

How To Copy

It's easy to think copying is just watching the greats, but do you know what you should be looking for when you set out to copy someone? Some young athletes believe all they have to do is pick someone, copy their skills and everything is good. They think it's just a copy and paste thing, but they are wrong. There is more to the process than just picking some successful person and starting. One of the most important things to consider when you are picking the person you want to copy is if they are the same type of athlete you are.

For instance, if Kobe would have chosen to copy Kareem Abdul-Jabbar, he might not have had the same results. Kareem is a very different athlete than Kobe. Although Kobe probably could have mastered the sky hook, playing with his back to the basket probably wouldn't have worked out so well for a 6′ 6″ guard. He even talked about wanting to copy Magic, but once he realized that he wasn't going to be 6′8″ like his dad he switched to Michael Jordan because he was more similar in body type. Those are Kobe's words.

So, how do you pick a good athlete to copy? First you make sure they play the same position you play, or at least a comparable position. Next look at their body type. Make sure their body type is the same as or similar to yours.

Find out how your idol, or person you choose to copy, does EVERYTHING. Learn how they challenge their fears. Learn how they train, think and stand up when they get knocked down. After you discover how they do all of these things, incorporate as many of them as you can into your daily routine as an athlete.

Congratulations! You Are Almost Finished!

We are almost at the end of the book! You only have two short chapters left. We have gone over a lot so far, so let's take a quick look back. Here's what you learned!

Eating The Frog

Eating the frog is doing your hardest or most taxing task first every day. We put it first because... well, I think you know why. Do the hard stuff first every day. Win the day at the beginning of the day.

Sacrificing

You will only get out what you put in. I could say that a lot of times in different ways, but that's basically the whole idea in a nutshell. If you want great things, you are going to have to put a lot into getting them. You will have to sacrifice.

Finding A Mentor

This is something you can do physically or virtually. Both are available to you in today's world thanks to the Internet. Find one and turn to them often. They can guide you to where you want to go a lot faster than you can by yourself.

Getting 1% Better

The compound effect of getting just 1% better every day is the game-changer all athlete's need to become legendary. Seems simple, but it's still one of the most underutilized tools of the trade. Improving by 1% every day will make all the difference.

Trash-Talking (Speaking Things into Existence)

This is only controversial because many don't understand its true intention. Now that you do, use it as a vocal manifestation, life creation technique.

Studying Film

As you know, you can use film study as a great tool to copy other greats. By watching them, you can practice the moves and skills you see them do and add them to your game.

Knowing Your History

Remember, not everything will apply to today's game. Make sure you take what works and discard the rest. That's how the greats before you became great! That's how the game grows and evolves. A lot of people have done what you want to do. They have struggled and failed at things along the way. Do yourself a favor and don't struggle with the same things that they struggled with. They are telling you how to avoid them. The idea is to skip those problems and roadblocks and encounter new ones. Move a little further down the road so you can move a little further down your road to success.

Copying Like Kobe

Copying the greats means taking what worked for them, learning it, then adding your own flair to it. Add your personal touch and modify it to suit your personality, ability and playing style. That is the best way to utilize creativity—not trying to be exactly like someone else and not attempting to create something from thin air. As Picasso said,

"Good artists borrow. Great artists steal!"

Have you ever wondered why biographies and autobiographies of most successful people become bestsellers? It's because people know the importance of learning from people who have walked the path. By reading their stories, people learn how these people went about gaining their success. Deep down, we all like to hear how people made it to the top. No reason why you shouldn't do the same!

Chapter Summary

- It is a great practice to copy someone who have excelled in the sport.

- Copying works because most of our problems are the same—and so are their solutions.

- When copying someone, ensure they have been successful in your sport.

CHAPTER 10

Who Is Responsible?

"Everything in your life is a reflection of a choice you have made. If you want a different result, be willing to make a different choice."

—Anonymous

(Parent/Coach Perspective)
Take Responsibility for Everything!

Gritty people know they are responsible for everything in their lives. If things go well, they are responsible. If things go poorly, they are responsible. No matter what happens, they always take responsibility for EVERYTHING that happens in their life—not their mom, not their dad, not society, not their coach. They are responsible. Their mantra is, "If it is going to be, it is up to me." If you are looking for excuses for why this didn't happen or why that didn't happen, you will always find one. You can always find someone or something to blame. That's the easy way out.

That's why a lot of people do it. Gritty people stop with that person in the mirror.

I didn't get a starter spot on my team because of this... I didn't make the team because of that... People sleeping on me because of the other thing...

Some people have a memorized list of things that are stopping or have stopped them from succeeding. They do that so they won't look too bad to their friends and themselves. They blame things around them but never seem to find a way to blame themselves. Most people forget that some other person is doing better despite having tougher circumstances and conditions than they have had. You can't tell them that, though. They would rather say it's the economy, the government, their birth conditions, some unlucky this or some unlucky that.

Okay. Let's have a real moment here. You have to realize that it is not what happens to you that determines how your life turns out, it's your response to what happens to you. Bad stuff happens to everybody. No matter how bad your bad is, another person's bad can be even worse. However, that doesn't mean you are not responsible for making your own situation better. The sunshine and the rain come down on all of us. Two people may find themselves in the same situation and come out with different outcomes.

It is not what happens to you that decides your outcome; it is what you do with what happens to you. If you are not having the success you want, you are not responding to the events around you in a way that creates success.

A wise person once said, **"If it's important, you will find a way, but if it is not, you will find an excuse."** Preach, sistah. PREACH! We all have our different struggles as human beings. All the rich people you see today have their stories of hard times to tell. They all have had their struggles. We all have our struggles. That is what being alive means. Society often only reminds us about the successes but ignores or minimizes and even forgets that there was a lot of pain that came with that success happy meal.

Storytime!

The Tale of Two Salesmen

Two salesmen wake up one morning and see that it is raining outside. The first salesman looks out of the window and says, *"What a storm! This is crazy! Nobody is going to work today. No need to make any sales calls. Nobody will be in the office with weather like this. I'll go make myself a coffee and enjoy the rest of the day, and maybe try again tomorrow."*

The second salesman looks out of the window and sees the same storm as the first guy. The lightning is flashing, and the rain is falling on his house as well. However, he has a different point of view. He thinks to himself, *What a storm! I bet a lot of salesmen will take the day off. Plus, a lot of other people will stay home because the storm is so crazy. That's great! I know exactly where to reach them. And since they are at home, they won't be working on anything so they will probably listen to my sales call now. Perfect opportunity for me to get out there and make some sales! Cha-ching!!*

Same storm, different mindsets. Listen, the rain falls on both the rich and the poor, the hungry and the well-fed. In this case, it fell on two salesmen at the same time. The difference is that one of them saw the storm as an opportunity and took action. The other found a perfect excuse not to take any action. This scenario applies to everyone. You need to decide whether or not you are going to look at life like salesman number-one or like salesman number-two. It really is that simple.

At the end of the day anyone who does not succeed in life has got to look themselves in the mirror and ask, "Why didn't it work out?"

1. Jim Rohn

Jim is one of my favorite speakers. He's a very straightforward, old-school kind of guy. This guy tells it like it is. According to him, accepting responsibility is the highest form of human authority. He believes the highest form of wisdom is accepting full responsibility for everything. How do you know you have made a transition from childhood to adulthood? It happens the day you take responsibility for your actions. Excuses are never hard to come by. Taking responsibility is a lot more difficult. Most people decide to take the easy route. Hey, I get it. Who wants to choose the hard way? However, at the end of the day, that is the way to ultimate success. Like we said before, with great reward will come great sacrifice

When someone wants an excuse to not be great at something, they will have no problem finding a lot of them. Excuses are readily available. *I'm not as tall as the players I see on t.v. I'm not as athletic,.*

When making excuses, these people fail to see that there are other people who have faced the same adversity but have taken the responsibility to make their mark on the sport. Whenever you feel the urge to start blaming people or things around you, always remember that *you* are the first reason for your success and your failure. That is the first step to taking responsibility like a BAWSE.

Murphy's Law states, "If anything can go wrong, it will!" So, what goes wrong should not be your focus. Get over it. No...*Grit* over it. Something will always go wrong along the way. The difference will always be in what you *do* about what went wrong.

2. Oprah Winfrey

Everybody knows Oprah Winfrey. She's a very popular American television producer, author, actress, talk show host and philanthropist. She didn't have the best childhood. But even at a very young age, she realized that she was responsible for how her life turned out. The cavalry wasn't coming, so she bought her own horse and rode it off into the sunset. *(Literally, she has her own horse farm.)* She was the person she had been waiting for.

Another person in the same situation probably would have believed that since they had a tough time growing up, it was impossible for them to make something out of life. In fact, a lot of people do that every day. Oprah made the decision to take responsibility. In her own words, she says,

"You are responsible for your own life. So, if you are sitting around, waiting for somebody to save you, fix you, or even help you, you are wasting your time because only you have the power to take responsibility to move your life forward."

Forget and forgive yourself for the past, face the present, take responsibility, and step into you're your new, amazing future!

3. Eric Thomas

Eric Thomas is an American motivational speaker and author. He's written several motivational books that have helped to inspire countless young people. In one of his presentations, he said the biggest problem most people have is wanting others to make guarantees to them when they are not willing to make a guarantee to themselves. Have you ever looked in the mirror and said, "I am the reason I am not on the next level?" Manyt people try to blame it on someone else or something outside of themselves.

As we have said before, the problem is always you, and on the flip side, the solution is always you. The sooner you realize this, the sooner you realize you can do better, and you can be better.

4. Michael Phelps

Michael is the American swimmer with the most Olympic medals in history, a total of twenty-eight. He wasn't just born one of the greatest Olympians in history. He practiced for eight hours every single day, including on his birthdays, for years. Every day. Not some days with weekends off; 365 days a year for years. That kind of focus and responsibility got him where he is today. Everybody sees him as the best, but not everybody is willing to go to the depths he was willing to go to in order to take responsibility for his athletic future.

Taking responsibility is all about making little steps in the right direction. A lot of people want to be successful, but a lot of people don't want to spend hours on the practicing part. Yes, you might be born with natural talents, but without putting in the work, without taking full control of what you do with your talent, there is little to no chance you will make and reach your goals.

Greatness is in everybody. Errbody. The issue is that very few people are willing to do what it takes to bring out that greatness. There are no excuses in life. Actually, there are a lot of excuses in life, just not any that get you anywhere you want to be. If you want to be the best, you need to take responsibility for your life and get to work. The only person stopping you is you.

Taking responsibility is the only way to see oneself through those tough times. Instead of feeling guilty for whatever position you are in, take little steps in the direction of your goals every day. Say to yourself, *"I am going to change this situation. I do not need any help because I have all the help I need right here inside of me."*

Like the great saying goes: Success is like a breath of air; although your last breath of air is important, it's not nearly as important as the next one. Wake up in the morning before you step onto that court or field and say the words, *"I am going to win. I am the victor, not the victim."*

Osho, an Indian mystic and founder of the Rajneesh movement believes people have failed to take responsibility because they have been taught to be dependent. If you have grown up avoiding responsibility, you will definitely reach a phase in your life when you need to change that. When this time of responsibility comes a lot of people start making excuses and blaming others. Long story even longer, DON'T do that!

I mean, you can do whatever you feel like doing, but bear one thing in mind: You are responsible for your actions *and* their consequences. Whether you like it or not. If you take the responsibility and move in the right direction, you will reap the benefits and if you don't take responsibility for yourself you won't get anywhere. Make the right choice, take control, and be better. Okay time to break it down. All you need to do is remember these five points.

- Do not blame others. No matter what happens, you must own everything you do or do not do.

- Be truthful with yourself. You need to give up all the excuses and start taking real action. It only takes 1%!

- Know you always have a choice. A wise man once said, "Action springs not from thoughts, but from a readiness for responsibility." Knowing that it is your choice to be where you are today will make you take charge of moving yourself forward.

- Refuse to complain. Always try to live in the moment. If it does not work out, do not dwell in the past. MOVE ON! Take another step in the right direction.

- Finally, ask yourself, **"What am I doing to take responsibility for my life right now?"** When you make the decision to take responsibility, things begin to change for the better. Every successful person in life made a conscious decision to take ownership of their life. How it turned out made them successful. Taking responsibility is where it all begins. If you want to live happily and successfully, take responsibility. Have I said that enough times in this chapter? Did I drill it into your head? It's not a one-time thing; it's an "every minute of your life" type of action.

Everything you do or don't do is a conscious decision made by you. It is up to you to make decisions that will point you in the direction of your dreams. Always remember that you are both the hero and the villain, the yin and the yang.

Going forward, tell yourself that you'll be the person in charge of everything that happens in your life.

Chapter Summary

- Taking responsibility determines how your life will turn out.

- The rain falls on everyone. It's not the rain, it's how you respond to it. Get an umbrella and a raincoat and keep it moving.

- Whenever you take action and it does not turn out as you'd hoped, accept it and believe it is in your hands to make things better next time.

- You owe *YOU!*

CHAPTER 11

Outwork Everyone

"Success isn't always about greatness. It's about consistency. Consistent hard work leads to success. Greatness will come."

- Dwayne "The Rock" Johnson

(Player Perspective)

Last but not least, OUTWORK EVERYONE! Before we go any further, let me say that it has been an honor to serve you all and to share this stuff with you. Our only hope in writing all of this is that it helps you become the best you can be at everything you do. Many of you we will never meet, however, both my dad and I are honored that, in some way, we helped you reach your greatest potential. Thank you for allowing us to be a small part of your journey!

That being said, it's time to get to work wrapping this all up! I would like to start this chapter with a story about Kobe Bryant. It is told best by the witness himself. Although there are millions of stories about Kobe's work ethic, this one was really cool. Enter, Jason Williams...

In this story, Jason gives a little backstory about how he normally went to the gym hours before the game even started. When he arrived at the gym, his routine was to make at least 400 practice shots before heading to the sauna to sit and wait for the game.

On this particular day, his team was scheduled to play Kobe and the Lakers. As the story goes, Jason got out of the car, walked into the arena and headed towards the basketball court to warm up. As he entered the players area of the arena, he heard a ball bouncing. Someone was already working out. He entered the gym, and there was Kobe Bryant. Bryant was already in a full sweat. He wasn't doing practice shots, he was going all out. Williams himself set up, put on his sneakers and began his typical pre-game workout. After working for more than an hour and a half, Jason felt that he was warmed up enough for the game. He sat down on the bench, unlaced his shoes and watched Kobe work out. Eventually, he got up and went to take a shower. Kobe had been working out before Jason got there, and he was still going after Jason was finished.

Jason couldn't believe it. He couldn't understand why Kobe would have to work so hard, especially on game day. Keep in mind that Kobe was already drenched in sweat before Jason arrived. Why would anyone want to work themselves out this much right before a game? Jason expected that Kobe would at least slow his pace due to tiredness. However, that wasn't the case for Kobe. He was doing serious game moves full-out in his pre-game workout. Jason became intrigued by the deliberate release of energy and the vigorous workout. After a while, Kobe stepped off of the court and went to the Laker lockeroom.

That night, Kobe scored 40 points. At the end of it all, Jason wasn't so interested in the game as much as he was in the volume of work he had seen Kobe put in. He couldn't get it out of his head. He saw Kobe work out like a maniac before the game then score forty points. He walked up to Kobe and asked the Mamba, "Hey, Kobe. Why were you in the gym for so long?"

Kobe said, "I saw you come in, and I wanted you to know that it doesn't matter how hard you work. It's that I am willing to work harder than you." Kobe wasn't done. He added, "You inspire me to be better." That's what all of this is about. We hope we've inspired you to be better.

Kobe's response made Williams think a lot afterward. It changed the course of his career from that moment on. It was the first time he saw a whole new level of competitiveness. He knew in that moment that he needed to start doing more. Before then, he had probably felt he was putting more than enough energy into basketball. However, his eyes were opened to the fact that…**"There are levels, kid."**

Williams also tells a story about how he got a tattoo on his hands that says *Believe.* His mom told him to believe in himself. She said, "If you don't believe in yourself, then who else is going to believe in you?" Boy, is that ever the truth. If you don't believe in yourself, don't expect others to believe in you. BELIEVE IN YOURSELF! YOU GOT THIS! YOU ARE ALREADY ELITE BECAUSE YOU HAVE ELITE INFORMATION.

Though Jason didn't see it as a good thing at the time, later in his life, Jason considered it a good thing that he felt like he was an overlooked athlete when he was a kid. It made him keep his head down and work even harder to be recognized.

10,000 Hours

You may or may not be familiar with the 10,000 hour principle. The idea is that it takes 10,000 hours to master a skill. The idea was popularized by Malcolm Gladwell in his bestseller, *Outliers: The Story of Success.* In his book, he talked about how research done at Berlin University showed that the most accomplished students had spent an average of 10,000 hours studying. He noted that Bill Gates spent an estimated 10,000 hours on programming work before he founded Microsoft. Gladwell also estimated that in the 1960s, The Beatles put in 10,000 hours of practice playing in Hamburg bars, and that Michael Jordan put in 10,000 hours of basketball. Kobe probably put in 10,001 'cause…Kobe.

From this research, the idea of putting in 10,000 hours to become an expert was born. We're bound to get better at something if we keep doing it. Especially if we do it for 10,000 hours. To be better than average, you have to put in more than average work. The issue is that people see the work needed as extra work instead of required work. Do the required work and the rest will fall into place.

We talked about this earlier, but in an interview, Mark Cuban was asked why he thinks people fail, and his one-sentence answer was, "Lack of brain power and lack of effort." That basically means lack of information and lack of application.

When people fail to make the effort, they don't learn. When people fail to learn, they take the wrong actions or put forth the wrong effort. He went on to explain that when you walk into a room for the first time, you are surrounded by competitors. There's no world in sports or business where there's no competition. None. If there's competition, that suggests someone else knows your business or sport either on the same level or a higher level.

If they know more about your sport than you do, you are probably going to lose. If you want to defeat your competitors, you've got to do the required work. A lot of athletes outwork their competition through education. When you know the game like we are talking about in this book, you give yourself a competitive advantage. Like we talked about before, most young athletes don't watch film and don't know their history. Sure, you can survive through middle school sports and possibly even play high school games, but when it comes to going to the next level they get left behind. Don't let that be you.

Outwork everyone, even when it comes to the mental part of the work. Be obsessed! Obsession is a word that gets used a lot when it comes to working your rear end off, but that is because people aren't really familiar with the amount of work needed to be considered to be obsessed! Pretty much every icon is said to have an insane work ethic. But maybe it's not an insane work ethic. Maybe it's just what is required to be great! Put that in your pipe and smoke it, as we used to say back in the day.

As you move into the realm of being obsessed about something, don't forget that being obsessed means gaining knowledge too. Don't just be a physical workout addict. Be a knowledge addict as well. Always look to absorb more experience and more information. We live in the information age, for goodness' sake. That's how you outwork your competition Mamba-style. There will always be that one person who will be ready to run the extra laps, do the extra push-ups or take the extra dive practices, but the line is always drawn and passed when you decide to do the mental work too. Take advantage of your advantages. As of this moment you have the advantage. I know I'm preaching to the choir by now, but I had to say it one more time.

Why can't it be you locked in the library, buried under a ton of books about your sport for hours? Why can't it be you running around the field for extra hours after everyone else has gone home? Why shouldn't it be you on the Internet doing research while everyone is laying their head on their pillows, snoring in the dark? Why can't it be you paying to learn a skill or taking a course?

It can be you, and it should be you. Do like Will Smith said, and just decide. Make the resolution, commit to the focus and intention to be better, and outwork the best in your field. The future belongs to those who can handle the pain and pressure. The future belongs to those disciplined enough to do more.

Natural abilities and talents are terrific, but clearly, they are not enough. You need to sharpen your skills and consciously continue to grow your work ethic and your mind. You will easily fly past all of the competition by outworking them. A good rule of thumb is to take what you think is a good amount of work and multiply it by ten, then you might be getting close. It always takes a lot more than you think that it's going to take. Always!

Chapter Summary

- Don't hate your competitors; let them motivate you to work harder and smarter.

- Beyond talent and natural ability, take extra time to work on your skills.

- The principle of putting 10,000 hours into your work is one that will help you outsmart your competitors easily.

CHAPTER 12

Final Thoughts

You made it to the end! Most people don't make it to the end of the books they buy. Just by completing this book, you are already showing that grit is a part of who you are! Nice work! Grit is a skill that is learned, and you just learned about all of its building blocks. Grit is a mental muscle that should be worked on and strengthened every day. Now you know how to do just that!

Let's go over what we learned so that you have it all fresh in your mind before you put this thing down and get to work. This has definitely been a deep dive, and your head might be spinning a little bit right now. It was a lot! Remember, all the stories from the greats we talked about are over on the free download. You can find it at mentaltoughnesspdf.com!

Eat The Frog

If you don't apply anything you learned in this book, make sure you do this one thing. We all have a habit of jumping on our phones or computers first thing in the morning. Don't do that anymore! When you do this, you are wasting prime-time brain power on meaningless tasks. Instead, be like the most accomplished who have learned how to focus and keep their attention on the big goals first thing in the morning. Do that!

Win the day first thing in the morning. Mentally strong people don't *think* they *might* succeed; they *know* they *will* succeed because before everyone else gets up, they eat their frog . Whether you want to drop a bad habit, run a marathon or do great in school, know that you can achieve anything you want if you commit to starting your day with a huge frog for breakfast.

Sacrifice To the Gods of Success

You can only get out of something what you put in. If you want something great, you are going to have to sacrifice greatly. The question is, "How badly do you want what you say you want?" The one thing I hope you got from this section of the book is that you can't sacrifice what everyone else thinks is reasonable and have what everyone else thinks is unreachable. That really is all there is to it. You are going to have to sacrifice greatly for great results. Decide if you want it that badly, and if you do, make sure your sacrifice matches your goal.

Who's Your Richard Williams?

You are going to want to have somebody around you who will hold your feet to the proverbial fire. Find your Richard Williams, even if it is a virtual mentor. In any situation, you'll be able to ask yourself what your mentor would suggest you do. Whether you have an in-person or virtual mentor, make sure you ask for their advice without reservation.

In soccer, there are defenders, attackers, midfielders and strikers helping each other achieve success. In baseball, you have outfielders that help the pitchers succeed. All of our examples of gritty athletes had a main someone, or a team of someones, for support. Your team doesn't have to be large, but it has to be present. Make sure you find a mentor. Work hard so you can be the perfect mentee. When the student is ready, the teacher will appear.

The 1% Rule

Focus on getting just one percent better every day. Don't try to eat the whole cow in one sitting, as they say. If you did ten push-ups yesterday, do ten and a half today. That's actually more than one percent, but you get the idea. If increasing by just half of a push-up is more than what you need to improve one percent, you can see exactly how little it takes to do this exercise. Trying to do half of a push-up might seem silly, but that is literally how little you have to improve each day. Do this one little thing and you are winning!

Talk Like Ali

Speak your desired reality into existence. This is the art of trash-talking. It's saying with passion what you want to happen. It's saying with passion what you want to be true.

Some people do it out loud, and some people do it internally, but everybody with grit does it and does it right . A lot of people don't know why the old-school guys did it, so they use it incorrectly. Now that you know what it is meant for, make sure to bring this part of the mental game into your game. It's super necessary.

Know Your History

Learn about the history of your sport. I can't tell you how easy this is but how few athletes do it. If you want to be one of the best to ever do it, learn your history. There is so much knowledge in the past. There are so many cheat codes that are waiting to be used. However, most people don't even try to discover them. You'll be surprised at how few will have the information you will gain from knowing your history. As someone who knows the history of their profession, let me tell you this: When you take the time to learn your history, you are going to find that you are playing chess while everyone else is playing checkers. Play chess, my friend. Play chess.

Copy Like Kobe

Pablo Picasso said, "Good artists borrow; great artists steal." Bruce Lee said, "Take what works and leave the rest." Somebody else said, "Don't try to reinvent the wheel." Somebody already went through the trouble of creating the wheel. They went through the failures and trials that it took to make the dang thing roll. Don't start from scratch; just put some rims on that mug! Copy like Kobe, Jordan, Pelé, Serena and Tyson. Find someone who is similar to you, copy their success, then add some of your own spice to it.

Take Responsibility

Take responsibility for everything. When things go well, it is your fault. When things go poorly, you are responsible. No matter what the outcome is, take responsibility for the things that happen in your life. Taking responsibility is key to all success. Take responsibility for EVERYTHING!

Outwork Everyone

I love how Kobe said that it truly is a game of time. Put in more time than anyone else and you win. The more you do, the better you do. Commit to an extreme work ethic and work more than everyone else. The rule of thumb for measuring this accurately is to take what you think is necessary and multiply it by ten. Then you might be close to knowing the amount of work that is needed to be great on the level that you want to be great. Outwork everyone.

Bonus!
Get rid of your self-limiting beliefs.

Self-limiting beliefs are the enemy. Thinking thoughts like...

I don't think I can do it.

I have no experience.

I will fail.

I've been unsuccessful before; I don't want to repeat the same mistake.

Will keep you from reaching your highest potential. Here's what I suggest you do: **Stop worrying about what other people will think, do and say.**

The real reason you are afraid of failing is because you are afraid of what other people will think. Who cares what they think? You have goals to reach. There will always be doubters and haters. The path to success is paved with failures. As Will Smith says, "FAIL EARLY, FAIL OFTEN, FAIL FORWARD!" Don't give them power over you by acknowledging their words, thoughts or negative energy. Stay focused on yourself and stop worrying about anybody else. Be willing to fail a lot, and fail faster.

Replace self-limiting beliefs with affirmations like...

I know I can do it, I just need to learn more or work more, and I will get the hang of it.

Just because I failed last time doesn't mean I will fail this time.

It doesn't matter what other people think.

It really is a game of you vs. you! Keep moving forward. The rest doesn't matter!

The Wrap-Up

Now comes the hard part. Don't just read this book and let it go to waste. Apply what you have learned. Do what we talked about. Your new gritty self is around the corner if you do. Remember, being gritty is a crucial asset everyone needs in all areas of their lives. Being gritty is essential for athletes and non-athletes if we are being honest. It's something you need in life no matter what you do.

We learned from greats like Kobe Bryant, The Rock, Serena Williams, Mike Tyson, Will Smith and many others. Now, apply what you have learned. It's one thing to read about it, but it's another thing to put the ideas into practice. You won't be great at it at first, and that's okay. Keep going until you are. Practice like a baby, remember?

Reading this book and making it just another addition to your library collection without practicing what you've learned would defeat the purpose of the book. We want to see action. We want someone to write a book about grit and add your story one day. Go and use what you have learned. Oh, and don't forget to get your free download. It's still out there waiting for you. You can find it at mentaltoughnesspdf.com.

We believe in you. We know you can do this. Now you have the tools to make it happen. Go and reach your goals! They are waiting for you. See you in the gym.

One Last Thing...

If you enjoyed this book or found it useful, I'd be very grateful if you'd post a short review on Amazon. Your support really does make a difference and I read all the reviews personally so I can get your feedback and make this book even better.

If you'd like to leave a review, then all you need to do is click the review link on this book's page on Amazon here: https://bit.ly/gritbookreview

Thanks again for your support!

ARE YOU READY FOR THE NEXT LEVEL?

FIRST: You need to make sure to listen to our free podcast episodes for athletes at http://hoopchalk.com/ Those episodes were super fun to record. Plus, they have a lot of information in them. You're gonna love them.

SECOND: Make sure that you pick up the book that started it all! This book is the foundation of everything that we learned! You are going to want this book if you don't already have it. Pick up your copy today!

Mental Toughness For Young Athletes

Click The Link Below To Take It To The Next Level

Mental Toughness For Young Athletes Volume 2: GRIT

Mental Toughness For Young Athletes:

Parent's Guide

Just Click The Link To Get Your Copy
Mental Toughness For Young Athletes – Parent's Version

Other Books By Moses And Troy Horne

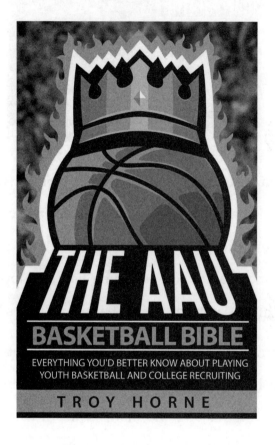

Click The Link Below To Take Your Youth Basketball Journey To The Next Level
The AAU Basketball Bible: Everything You'd Better Know About Youth Basketball And College Recruiting

About The Authors

Moses Horne is a High School basketball player who started playing basketball in the 5th grade. He has interviewed Kobe Bryant, Jason Richardson, Earl Boykins, and many other NBA Vets and players. He has even had the opportunity to workout with and get tips from Chauncey Billups himself.

On his journey he learned a lot from the greats. They not only taught him the physical game, they also taught him the mental game. In this book he shares some of what he learned with you! This is the only book out there with input and information from an actual youth player.

You can follow his journey on…

Instagram: https://www.instagram.com/moforeal05/

Twitter: https://twitter.com/moforeal05

 **Troy Horne** is a dad who knew nothing about the sport of basketball except that his son wanted to grow up to play the sport professionally. As a former professional musician, Broadway star, and television actor he had a hypothesis. That hypothesis was that certain truths held fast in all professional industries. He believed that the staples of work hard, master your skills, meet the right people, and put yourself in the right places were not only essential for the music business but essential for all professions. So he went in search of the information that he thought that he would need to help his son Moses reach his basketball goals and dreams. Along the way, they ran into the *Mental Toughness Roadblock*.

Mental Toughness For Young Athletes: Eight Proven 5-Minute Mindset Exercises For Kids And Teens Who Play Sports... is a collection of exercises that he found to help his young athlete conquer the feelings of nervousness and sports anxiety in high-pressure situations. These exercises gained from talking with Elite College Athletes, NBA Veterans and

College Coaches on their podcast (Hoopchalk Basketball Podcast) have been game-changers in mentally difficult situations. These short but effective mind gym workouts edited just for young athletes have been life-changing when it comes to high performance. See you on the inside.

References

Born, S. (2005). *15 Simple Ways to Improve Your Athletic Performance Right Now*. Retrieved from Hammer Nutrition: https://www.hammernutrition.com.au/info-centre/15-simple-ways-to-improve-athletic-performance-right-now/

Connecticut, U. o. (2019, July 25). *'Trash talk' really can put players off their game*. Retrieved from Science Daily: https://www.sciencedaily.com/releases/2019/07/190725112555.htm

Do, C. (2020, April 24). *How to Boost Your Confidence*. Retrieved from the Futur: https://thefutur.com/blog/boost-self-confidence-emulate-someone

Elderkin, P. (1987, August 6). *Mark my words: McGwire could be the next Babe*. Retrieved from The Christian Science Monitor: https://www.csmonitor.com/1987/0806/rmark.html

Clear, J. (n.d). The 1 Percent Rule: Why a Few People Get Most of the Rewards. Retrieved from James Clear Blog:

https://jamesclear.com/the-1-percent-rule#:~:text=The%201%20Percent%20Rule%20states,need%20to%20be%20slightly%20better.

Clear, J. (n.d). *Continuous Improvement: How It Works and How to Master It.* Retrieved from James Clear Blog https://jamesclear.com/continuous-improvement

Jason. (2016, March 22). *The 5 Hardest Working Athletes to Motivate You to Keep Trying.* Retrieved from LegitGambling: https://www.legitgamblingsites.com/blog/hard-work-do-you-train-as-hard-as-these-5-athletes/

John, A. S. (2017, January 28). *Is Richard Williams, Serena and Venus's Dad, The Greatest Coach Of All Time?* Retrieved from Forbes: https://www.forbes.com/sites/allenstjohn/2017/01/28/is-richard-williams-serena-and-venuss-dad-the-greatest-coach-of-all-time/?sh=737f14f56431

Kaish, A. (n.d). *The 1% Rule That'll Make Reaching Big Goals Feel Easy.* Retrieved from The Muse: https://www.themuse.com/advice/the-1-rule-thatll-make-reaching-big-goals-feel-easy

Kullah, P. (2016, July 31). *1% a day makes you 37 times better in a year*. Retrieved from Medium https://medium.com/life-maths/life-maths-1-change-a-day-make-you-37-times-better-in-1-year-eeb66db70120

Lacerda, C. (2020, July 12). *Create Your Ideal Life with the 1 Percent Rule*. Retrieved from Medium: https://medium.com/@ceciliaalacerda/create-your-life-with-the-1-percent-rule-9b22a83a921d

Lee, C. (2019, March 29). *Athletes see, athletes do: watching sports benefits athletes' performance*. Retrieved from The Epic: https://lhsepic.com/4989/sports/athletes-see-athletes-do-watching-sports-benefits-athletes-performance/#:~:text=Watching%20a%20professional%20play%20the,believe%20in%20their%20own%20skills.

Pawan. (2019, September 10). *Don't copy, emulate*. Retrieved from Medium: https://medium.com/@coffeebytwo/emulate-dont-just-copy-3039ea2a544

Rafael, D. (2016, June 6). *Muhammad Ali continues to inspire boxing's next generation*. Retrieved from ESPN:

Mental Toughness for Young Athletes

https://www.espn.com/boxing/story/_/id/15951923/fighters-young-old-draw-inspiration-muhammad-ali

Rumora, E. (n.d.). *Emulating Others on the Way to Business Success*. Retrieved from BusinessCollective: https://businesscollective.com/emulating-others-on-the-way-to-business-success/index.html

Seekins, B. (2016, June 14). *Ranking Muhammad Ali's 10 Greatest Lines of Trash Talk*. Retrieved from Bleacher Report: https://bleacherreport.com/articles/2645884-ranking-muhammad-alis-10-greatest-lines-of-trash-talk

Spears, M. (2016, June 13). *The unwritten rules of trash talk*. Retrieved from The Undefeated: https://theundefeated.com/features/lebron-james-and-trash-talk/

Staff, T. (2020, May 1). *NBA lookback: Kobe Bryant breaks Michael Jordan's NBA All-Star Game scoring record*. Retrieved from Chicago Tribune: https://www.chicagotribune.com/sports/national-sports/sns-michael-jordan-kobe-bryant-last-dance-20200501-mtsp4m6nmvgpvokxt5jjo7ttca-story.html

Taylor, J. (2017, December 6). *Watching Video is Great Mental Training for Athletes*. Retrieved from Huffpost: https://www.huffpost.com/entry/watching-video-is-great-m_b_11427136

Team, A. (2017, November 15). *Can you guess the one thing that most elite athletes have in common?* Retrieved from Active For Life: https://activeforlife.com/what-elite-athletes-have-in-common/

9 3.